KAFKA *versus* KAFKA

KAFKA
versus
KAFKA

by

MICHEL CARROUGES

Translated by EMMETT PARKER

UNIVERSITY OF ALABAMA PRESS

University, Alabama

Table of Contents

Author's Preface
to the English Translation

Kafka and the Odyssey of Israel ...

Never before has the message of Kafka's work had a more vibrant and universal timeliness.

The state of Israel, after nineteen centuries, has been reborn like the Phoenix. It is not the first nation to rise out of its own ruins. But no other has ever suffered so long a period of annihilation or so widespread a dispersion—and yet survived. Israel is a specter of History, but one of flesh and bones, as a man returned from the dead.

Newspapers can tell us of the vicissitudes of Israel's long struggle to be reborn in the world of today. But what force has brought together from the four corners of the earth this new Israel, a nation risen up between Pharoah and Sennacherib?

The Bible itself is the initial key to the Jews' indestructible faith in their future. Judaic sacred literature, from the Talmudists to the Hasidists, reveals how that hope was sustained from ancient times until now.

This long ray of light, the hope that has been the guiding beacon of Jewish history, does not fully explain the phenomenon of Israel's rebirth. Looking at it alone, we are dazzled. Everything appears to be too simple and inevitable. We lose sight of the great shadowy labyrinths in which, before the dawn of liberation, the light of hope often seemed to be shrouded in an interminable midnight.

If there has been a single writer able to depict this shadowy labyrinth, this nocturnal side of the Jewish odyssey, with greater power than any other, it was certainly Franz Kafka. In his writings the irreal and the absurd are not merely secondary aspects that are ultimately integrated into an essentially coherent and realistic symbolism. If we take care not to forget the other meanings that are inherent in his symbolism, Kafka's work can legitimately be understood to represent an extraordinary Jewish odyssey that evokes the suffering of the Jews—wandering (*Amerika*), rejected (*The Castle*), unjustly accused (*The Trial*), tortured (*The Penal Colony*), etc.

As dark and inexorable as the shadows seem to be, the shadows that seek to possess the oppressed Kafkean hero, the writer struggles to survive and discovers somewhere—far away and very faint, but invincible—a gleaming pinpoint, a ray of light, an ultimate hope of justice, deliverance, and resurrection. In the black maze of anguish, hope never shines like the sun; it remains small, sometimes even hidden, and yet as unerring as the North Star.

Though steeped in Jewish culture, Franz Kafka was not a "practicing" Jew. It cannot even be said that he was a faithful believer in the God of Abraham. The atmosphere of his work and certain reflections uttered to his friends indicate rather that he was an agnostic, patiently rebellious with regard to a God who refused to come out from behind a wall of hypotheses to reveal His indifference and severity towards humanity. Kafka was as far from the God of Israel as he was from the Promised Land.

However, if all seemed lost in heaven, as well as on earth, hope survived everything.

During the last years of his life Kafka, along with his friends, showed great enthusiasm for the Zionist movement. He had dreams of founding a sort of kibbutz, and he even planned on several occasions to depart for the ancient homeland of his ancestors, which had just begun to open up after World War I. Thus he participated in the national, social, and humanitarian movement that prepared the way for the rebirth of the state of Israel after World War II.

But this is not all.

In Kafka's astonishing meditations on Abraham, Moses, Canaan, Paradise, we see to what extent he was haunted by the biblical sources of Jewish hopes. Despite the passing of centuries, despite all disasters, the point of light remained indestructible because it was unconditional. Agnostic and individualistic, Kafka was no less a mystic as well. He was passionately fascinated by the distant light that had led Abraham, Moses, and an entire people towards the Promised Land—towards that earthly figuration of the Paradise lost and the Paradise to come.

The accumulation of limitless sufferings and, simultaneously, the survival of the lodestar of hope is a secret common to the work of Kafka and to the odyssey of the Jewish people for nineteen centuries. At the same time, it illuminates for us the mystery and the reality of History: all that can be destroyed, can be brought back to life. There is surely no believer in the God of Abraham, Isaac, and Jacob—Jew or non-Jew—who will not be moved to the depths of his being by the universal value of such a message.

MICHEL CARROUGES

Paris, France
December, 1967

Kafka versus *Kafka*. Why? Because *The Trial* of Kafka, the writer and lawyer, is the trial of the son by the father, of the father by the son, and even of the son by the son. Woman, society, the human condition, and God Himself are also placed on trial. But the accuser never spares himself; he does not even spare himself the love of those whom he accuses of tearing him asunder.

KAFKA *versus* KAFKA

Abbreviations Used to Designate Works Quoted in The Text*

CWK = *Conversations with Kafka:* Gustav Janouch's record of his and Kafka's conversations, set down at the time of their relationship (1920–23).

DI = Franz Kafka: *Diaries: 1910–13.*

DII = Franz Kafka: *Diaries: 1914–23.*

DF = Franz Kafka: *Dearest Father.* This volume contains Kafka's "Letter to His Father," "Wedding Preparations in the Country," "Reflections on Sin, Suffering, Hope, and the True Way," "The Eight Octavo Notebooks," "Fragments from Notebooks and Loose Pages," and "Paralipomena."

FK = *Franz Kafka:* Max Brod's biographical study of Kafka's life and work.

*For more complete bibliographical data, see the Select Bibliography at the back of this book.

Introduction

The Gordian Knot . . .

Everything in Kafka's life and work is bound up together. Between what he did, what he dreamed, and what he wrote there are innumerable interrelationships.

In his diaries one finds—pell-mell—reflections, recollections, accounts of dreams, and short stories or fragments of novels. The surprising thing is that these in no way give the impression of bric-a-brac. On the contrary, as one begins reading a passage, one is not entirely sure whether it deals with an actual experience recalled, a reverie, or a work of fiction. Between each of these three planes there seems to exist no difference of tone, only one of degree. All of them form a single, continuous filament. It is not until the reader is well into an entry that he begins to sense on what plane the narrative takes place, depending on whether the view of reality is more or less fluid, more or less capricious. Even so, one cannot always be sure of the category into which a given passage falls.

In each case, the dominant tone is one of fantastic realism. Everything is realistic and strange, unusual and familiar. For contrary to a widely accepted point of view, there is nothing of the *un*realistic in Kafka. His descriptions of external everyday life, of the sort that we all lead, are admirable in their precision and vividness. They unmask the feeble routines that are so much a part of our prefabricated representations of daily life, biting into the very marrow of reality, revealing its disquieting strangeness. As though to compensate, Kafka's dreams appear much more coherent and closer to wide-awake experience than our own. In his short stories and novels—that is to say, in the activity that grew out of his wakeful dreams—it was only a matter of consolidating this double heritage in order to fuse it into a whole.

Ordinarily the three levels of psychic activity, wide-awake reflections, dreams that occur during sleep, and wakeful reveries or daydreams, interrelate only through the subterranean passages of the subconscious. With Kafka, however, one might say that they merge into unity on one single level.

For this to have occurred he must have been extraordinarily acute in the observation of images, and above all he must have suffered some deep psychic wound. For normally the compartments of the consciousness are not easily broken through, nor do they lend themselves to any degree of transparency without some rending asunder of the self. Kafka's lucidity is admirable, but it is only nascent, not sovereign; tragic, not harmonious. At every step this lucidity had to pay a heavier and heavier tribute of suffering, and even a ransom of blindness, for everything in this world has its price. If Kafka understood clearly what we do not understand, it is because he did not succeed in understanding what we understand—or think we understand. Kafka's lucidity has nothing in common with the facile insight of the clairvoyant. It is a lucidity born of suffering, heroically analyzed.

Begun in 1910, in Kafka's twenty-seventh year, the diaries mark the beginning of that long, ardent, frozen, half-desperate and yet unconquerable odyssey that was to sweep him along throughout his life.

"In the context of the diary," according to Max Brod, "there are also many fragments of short stories which have gone thus or thus far; they pile up, until suddenly out of the throng the first finished story of considerable length, 'The Verdict,'* shoots out like a jet of flame. With it, during the night of September 22–23, 1912, the writer succeeded in breaking through to the form that suits him, and a powerful genius of the art of story telling, unique in his genre, finally found his freedom" (*FK*, 106).

On the August 13 preceding, Kafka had met Felicia B., who was twice to be his fiancée. *The Judgment*, then, dates from two months later. He composed it in a single sitting, between ten in the evening and six in the morning, on that famous night of September 22–23.

Dedicated to F., this story knowingly plays upon the names of the tale's hero and heroine so as to render them analogous to Kafka's and Felicia's names (*DI*, 279). This link with real life is all the more intimate in that the story describes the combat between a son and his father over a fiancée, a combat that ends with the suicide of the son at the father's order.

Strange as this tale is, it reveals to us the even more astonishing strangeness of Kafka's struggle against his father, the initial key to all the other dramas of Kafka's life. In writing it, Kafka departed from the diary form to attain that of pure literary creation, but his intimate personal life continued to be projected into his work.

On every psychic level the year 1912 was a period of capital importance for Kafka. The hope for happiness shone so brightly that he began his first novel, *Amerika*, the only one that manifests a great spirit of playfulness and of departure for the "new world" in every sense of the word. He worked on it for a long time, yet he never succeeded in writing the last chapter, which was to have decided the happiness of his hero. Worse still, he interrupted this work, in 1912 or 1913, in order to write *The Metamorphosis*, that nightmare in which a man awakens changed into a vermin and dies rejected by all those around him.

* Entitled *The Judgment* in the Schocken edition [see *The Penal Colony* (New York, 1961), pp. 49–63]; this title will be used throughout the present study [trans. note].

Was there any less despair in Kafka's life as he progressively sank further and further into the morass of broken love affairs, and finally into the sickness that was to be the *coup de grâce* for him?

In July, 1914, Kafka broke with Felicia. The end of his first engagement took place in Berlin at a meeting between Kafka, Felicia, and the latter's parents. Felicia's father had traveled all night by train to come to the meeting—and there he sat in his shirtsleeves, in the hotel room where he was staying. "The tribunal in the hotel," Kafka called it (*DII*, 65). Indeed one can already recognize the atmosphere of *The Trial*, where the tribunal functions amid the clutter of household activities in a building that resembles a large, nondescript structure on the outskirts of the city, rather than a "Palace of Justice." Now, it was precisely in that same year, 1914, that Franz read to his friend Max Brod the first chapter of *The Trial*, in which the hero bears the initial K. and Felicia B. reappears as Fräulein Bürstner. In November, 1914, as in 1912, Kafka again interrupted work on his novel to write a nightmare tale: *The Penal Colony*, the story of a torture machine on which the officer who tends the machine eventually commits suicide. These two works, Brod declares, "are documents of literary self-punishment, imaginative rites of atonement" [*FK*, 146].

In 1917, Kafka renewed his relationship with Felicia. In vain, however, for he was to break up with her again, and for the last time, a few months later. In 1919, he had a second, ephemeral fiancée, Julie Wohryzek. And yet, as deeply as he was thus involved in the devastation of his personal life, Kafka seems to have found new hope in his meeting with Milena Jesenská in 1920. Despite the torments of their love, a certain renewal seems to be taking form in the third long novel that Kafka began writing at that time, *The Castle*. Between the obscure powers who reign from deep inside the castle and the solitary powerlessness of the appointment-seeking Land Surveyor, the only power of intercession lies with women; thus, it is ever the same tragedy that is evoked. One of the women is named Frieda, and according to Brod, her role in the novel presents more than one feature in common with that of Milena (*FK*, 220; cf. *CWK*, xvii).

But Milena was married, and despite the great freedom she enjoyed in her manner of living, she could not bring herself to leave her husband—and Kafka accepted her decision (*FK*, 231). Again Kafka never succeeded in writing the final chapter that was to conclude the fate of his alter ego in *The Castle*. In 1923, Kafka and Milena broke off their relationship forever.

We have only begun to explore the immense labyrinth of Kafka's life and works. The keys that he provides would not be sufficient if he had not given us that very first, most important key, the one that permits us to open the main gate into the labyrinth: the "Letter to His Father."

Beginning with *The Judgment*, the specter of Kafka's father was discernible in the person of the father who condemns his son to break his engagement by killing himself. There are those who will immediately protest that this is not believable. Others will tend to mistrust "instinctively" any enlightenment that psychoanalysis might provide—as if Kafka himself had not noted in his recollections of the night of September 22–23, 1912: ". . . thoughts about Freud, of course . . ." (*DI*, 276). Then there are those who will "systematically" discover, beneath the obscure forces that are at work in *The Castle*, *The Trial*, *The Penal Colony*, etc., the father's obsessive intervention.

But Kafka tolerated no easy evasions. He knew only too well the origin of the monstrous evil that gnawed at him; it was he himself who said to Max Brod that he would have liked to characterize his entire literary output " 'as an attempt to get away from my father' " (*FK*, 24).

Of course—and one rejoices at the fact—there are a thousand other things to be found in Kafka's writings, and to reduce the whole of his work to the level of a psychoanalytic document would be utterly ridiculous. The rose is not to be known by its root alone; but, by the same token, the rose does not deny its root. Kafka knew this as well as anyone, and better than most, as he demonstrated in November, 1919 when he wrote that monumental, 48-page letter destined for his father, in which he attempted to explain the causes of their conflict and its incalculable consequences for him.

Nothing can replace reading this invaluable letter, which relates in minute detail how as a child Kafka felt himself overpowered by his father, a feeling that continued through adolescence and adulthood—Kafka wrote the letter when he was thirty-six. Even at this age he had not achieved true emancipation; as he himself put it, he could not seize from his father his independence as a man without marrying and founding his own family, and yet it was precisely this overwhelming paternal obsession that inhibited his attempts to marry.

Such is Kafka's own explanation of the succession of broken engagements and of the haunted atmosphere of his work. Such clear insight into the self is astounding. But is the way in which the father sapped his son's vital energies any more readily conceivable?

However, out of failure itself Kafka achieved triumph, through the tremendous courage of his lucidity. If Franz had not existed no one today would remember Hermann Kafka. While the son thought himself overwhelmed by the father, the latter survives only through the son: Hermann Kafka has become entirely the creature of Franz Kafka.

Kafka, despite everything, succeeded in founding his "household" in the realm of art. There he begot his own father anew, exorcising him in the form of a monstrous ghost, a figure in the mythology of a body of work that the father could not even begin to understand. There could be no more bitter irony nor any more noble revenge.

Let us try now to penetrate further into the labyrinth.

1

The Struggle
Against the Father

In 1920, a year after Kafka had written the "Letter to His
Father," the young Gustav Janouch, who had greatly admired
Franz Kafka even before making his acquaintance, set down a
firsthand account of the following incident, which he had
witnessed one evening in Prague:

My first walk with Franz Kafka ended in the following way:
Our circuit of the [Altstädter] Ring had brought us back to the
Kinsky Palace, when from out of the warehouse, with the business
sign HERMANN KAFKA, emerged a tall, broad man in a dark
overcoat and a shining hat. He remained standing about five steps
away from us and waited.
As we came three paces nearer, the man said, very loudly:
"Franz. Go home. The air is damp."
Kafka said, in a strangely gentle voice:
"My father. He is anxious about me. Love often wears the face
of violence. Come and see me."
I bowed. Franz Kafka departed, without shaking hands (*CWK*,
31).

Some time later, Janouch saw Kafka, who had just returned
from a visit to the country, and said to him:

"So now we are at home again."
Kafka smiled sadly.
"At home? I live with my parents. That is all. It is true I have a

small room of my own, but that is not a home, only a place of refuge, where I can hide my inner turmoil, only in order to fall all the more into its clutches" (*CWK*, 40).

At that time, Franz, who was thirty-seven and a bachelor, was already suffering from tuberculosis, which explains his living at home and his father's urgent solicitude; but the tyranny inherent in this situation was none the less evident.

The situation, moreover, was very complicated, for Kafka's attitude was one neither of total rebellion nor of complete submission. Franz considered his father a superior type of man whom he envied and whom he found objectionable at the same time. He did not wish to be the kind of man his father was, and he could not have been.

In a letter written to F. B. in 1916 he strongly underlined the extreme ambivalence of his feelings:

However, I am descended from my parents, am linked to them and my sisters by blood, am sensible of it neither in my everyday affairs nor, as a result of their inevitable familiarity to me, in my special concerns, but at bottom have more respect for it than I realize. (*DII*, 167).

To which he immediately added:

Sometimes this bond of blood too is the target of my hatred; the sight of the double bed at home, the used sheets, the nightshirts carefully laid out, can exasperate me to the point of nausea, can turn me inside out . . . (*Ibid.*).

All that Kafka says about his love for his mother, his sisters, and even for his father can be found in the letter to his father. Never does Franz address Hermann in a tone of hatred, scorn, or even cold indifference. Rarely have such grave reproaches been expressed with such delicacy, such gentleness, and with such a desire not to offend someone who himself never ceased to offend. The son so scrupulously analyses his relations with his father that he stresses every possibility of interpretation that might justify his parent. Kafka felt everything deeply, yet he surmounted it all. The letter begins:

Dearest Father:
You asked me recently why I maintain that I am afraid of you. As usual, I was unable to think of any answer to your question, partly for the very reason that I am afraid of you, and partly because an explanation of the grounds for this fear would mean going into far more details than I could even approximately keep in mind while talking (*DF*, 138).

This opening suffices to set the tone of the whole letter written in 1919. Sometimes, when one misreads Kafka's novels, one finds them systematically long and interminable, indeed boring, because one judges things summarily. What one had thought to be simple, rapid, and clear, Kafka pitilessly reveals (primarily for himself, but for us also), as complex, broad in scope, and obscure. Thereby he teaches us to see what we did not previously know how to see. In the letter to his father, however, as on every occasion when he deems it well to do so—at the beginning of his novels, for example—he goes directly to the heart of the burning question.

How to understand that fear of his father? That is what he seeks to explain interminably, for the subject is indeed inexhaustible. The basis for that fear was his father's "intellectual domination" (*DF*, 145), a term oppressive in its meaning and, at the same time, filled with unspeakable irony:

You had worked your way up so far alone, by your own energies, and as a result you had unbounded confidence in your opinion . . . From your armchair you ruled the world. Your opinion was correct, every other was mad, wild, *meshugge*, not normal (*DF*, 145).

Kafka saw in his father the very "ideal" of the paterfamilias, the man who is capable of establishing a household, of governing his wife and children, of having a profession that enables him to feed his family and to make his way in society. In order to accomplish all this, he says:

What is essential . . . is what I have recognized in you, and indeed everything rolled into one, good and bad, as it is organically combined in you, that is to say, strength, and scorn of the other, health and a certain immoderation, eloquence and inadequacy, self-confidence and dissatisfaction with everyone else, a superior attitude to the world and tyranny, knowledge of human nature and mistrust of most people, then also good qualities without any drawback, such as industry, endurance, presence of mind, and fearlessness (*DF*, 192–93).

Kafka adds, however: "Of all this I had by comparison almost nothing or only very little . . ." (*Ibid.*).

Some might be inclined to conclude from the son's apology, ironic as it is, that his father was an extraordinary man, although, as Max Brod points out, Franz exaggerated his father's qualities. While this is quite evident, Kafka did not exaggerate the antinomy that existed between him and his father, if one tends to see their relationship in terms of the opposition between the man of affairs and the intellectual.

To begin let us turn back to Kafka's childhood memories. It is difficult to choose among the thousand telling details of the father's behavior at table, his methods of punishment, or his outbursts of anger at the store; they could be cited endlessly. It is perhaps of more importance to stress the father's imprecatory side, his long series of not so much pedagogical as Jupterian apostrophes:

Because in accordance with your strong appetite and your particular habit you ate everything fast, hot and in big mouthfuls, the child had to hurry, there was a somber silence at the table, interrupted by admonitions: "Eat first, talk afterwards" . . . Bones mustn't be cracked with the teeth, but you could. Vinegar must not be sipped noisily, but you could (*DF*, 148).

It was only necessary to be happy about something or other, to be filled with the thought of it, to come home and speak of it, and the answer was an ironical sigh, a shaking of the head, a tapping of the table with one finger: "Is that all you're worked up about?" . . . or "What can you buy yourself with that?" or "What a song and dance about nothing!" (*DF*, 146).

How terrible for me was, for instance, that "I'll tear you apart like a fish," in spite of knowing, of course, that there was nothing worse to follow (admittedly, as a little child I didn't know that), but it was almost exactly in accord with my notions of your power and I saw you as being capable of doing this too (*DF*, 152).

What was also maddening were those rebukes when one was treated as a third person, in other words accounted not worthy even to be spoken to angrily: that is to say, when you would speak in form to Mother but in fact to me, sitting there at the same time. For instance: "Of course, that's too much to expect of our worthy son" and the like (*DF*, 153).

Each incident, if one speaks only of isolated cases, amounted to no more than a drop of water, but as they accumulated, day after day, throughout the course of the years, they could no longer be considered as isolated. The single drops of water had become an ocean of bitterness; finally they became a tidal wave and catastrophe struck:

The impossibility of getting on calmly together had one more result, actually a very natural one: *I lost the capacity to talk* [my italics]. I dare say I would never have been a very eloquent person in any case, but I would, after all, have had the usual fluency of human language at my command. But at a very early stage you forbade me to talk. Your threat: "Not a word of contradiction!" and the raised hand that accompanied it have gone with me ever since. What I got from you—and you are, as soon as it is a matter of your own affairs, an excellent talker—was a hesitant, stammering mode of speech, and even that was still too much for you, and finally I kept silent, at first perhaps from defiance, and then because I couldn't either think or speak in your presence. And because you were the person who really brought me up, this has had its repercussions throughout my life (*DF*, 150–51).

Kafka wrote, in fact, as early as 1913, in a projected letter to Felicia B.'s father:

. . . I live in my family, among the best and most lovable people, more strange than a stranger. I have not spoken an average of twenty words a day to my mother these last years, hardly ever said more than a hello to my father. I do not speak at all to my married sisters and my brothers-in-law, and not because I have anything against them. The reason for it is simply this, that I have not the slightest thing to talk to them about. *Everything that is not literature bores me and I hate it* . . . [my italics] (*DI*, 299–300).

This last statement may seem surprising: some will insist that it reflects the egotism of the man of letters, the stale detachment

of the intellectual, the narcissism of the writer, and other phrases
of the same stamp that only serve to avoid confronting the real
issues. In fact, there is a tragic and intimate link between this
remark in the letter to Felicia's father and the brutally overwhelming statement revealing the catastrophe that had occurred
in Kafka's childhood world: "I lost the capacity to talk."
Aphasia, occurring mainly in the mind and in a relative sense of
the word, but aphasia nonetheless. For dialogue is a vital necessity, and an upbringing without dialogue between parent and
child can only be monstrous. Kafka was aware of this: between
the father and the son the barrier of silence grew higher, expanded indefinitely, and finally formed truly a "Great Wall of
China." In an ultimate assault Franz tried one day to open a
breach in the wall of silence, but only by means of a letter, a
letter he could not even mail or give to his father; he could only
give it to his mother, and she decided that it was impossible to
deliver it to its intended recipient. As in Kafka's writings, the
message can only come too late, after death. It is we, strangers,
who receive Kafka's message, which was not destined for us.
Out of the silence between father and son, like a poisoned spring,
flow other rivers of silence between Franz and his family, between Franz and the people he met, even between him and the
women he tried to love, because the distance between Kafka's
inner self and the exterior world had become too great.

There is another side to this silence, however. It is not the
empty silence of the yogi, but the overflowing silence of suppressed words, of sensitivity turned inward, of thoughts return-
ing endlessly to their source.

What in fact is an intimate diary such as Kafka's if not the
beach where one finds the flotsam and jetsam of suffering and the
treasures that the mainstream of life has rejected? What is literature, when it aims at something more than facile amusement or
commercialism, if not the inverse reflection of what life has produced and rejected? It is for that very reason that the work of
art produces a catharsis, that is to say, liberates, because it sur-

renders the body to phantoms that haunt the mind and projects these phantoms into the exterior world.

Happy peoples have no history; happy men do not make literature. At the source of literature, there can only be an initial wound that opens the interior world to the light. The spoken word when repressed, like the Divine Word, transforms shapeless shadows into light and into cosmos.*

If Kafka reveals to us today many secrets of the human consciousness, it is because he was capable of exorcising from his being immemorial prohibitions imposed by an inner sense of guilt. If he was capable of doing so, it was because he was forced in that direction by an illegitimate, external prohibition that hindered him from giving ordinary expression to his inner thoughts. But Hermann Kafka could not have foreseen this, no more than the Sultan could have imagined that in barring the route to the Indies, he "forced" Columbus to discover the New World.

Franz wrote to his father:

. . . You have a dislike in advance of every one of my activities and particularly of the nature of my interest . . . (DF, 175).

This applied to thoughts as well as to people. It was enough that I should take a little interest in a person—which in any case did not happen often, as a result of my nature—for you, without any consideration for my feelings or respect for my judgment, to butt in with abuse, defamation, and denigration. Innocent, childlike people, such as, for instance, the Yiddish actor Löwy, had to pay for that. Without knowing him you compared him, in a dreadful way that I have now forgotten, to vermin and as was so often the case with people I was fond of you were automatically ready with the proverb of the dog and its fleas** (DF, 146–47.)

---

* This is also why literature tends to create a "new" language, a private, secret language incomprehensible to the "father" and at the same time one that is ruminated over, reduced again and again in the crucible of the imagination.

** Wer sich mit Hunden niederlegt, steht mit Flöhen auf. Who lies down with dogs gets up with fleas [trans. note].

Nor was such behavior on his father's part limited to Kafka's young childhood or merely to friends. When Franz alluded to one of his proposed marriages, his father crushed him with sarcasm:

What you said to me was more or less as follows: "She probably put on some specially chosen blouse, the thing these Prague Jewesses are good at, and straightway, of course, you made up your mind to marry her. And, what's more, as fast as possible . . ." . . . You have, I suppose, scarcely ever humiliated me more deeply with words and have never more clearly shown me your contempt . . . Of my attempts to escape in other directions you knew nothing . . . and had to try and guess at them, and your guess was in keeping with your total judgment of me, a guess at the most abominable, crude, and ridiculous thing possible (*DF*, 187–88).

Kafka's heart was devastated. But this does not tell the whole story, for at the same time all that the heart gives life to was similarly devastated: all sense of life, all human relationships. Kafka's admirable intelligence could no longer reflect anything but an almost desperate, nocturnal world of ruins peopled by phantoms.

Yet, this heart was ceaselessly reborn intact, thirsting for love, incapable of blindness or hatred, never forgetting that there were hours in that hell that were at once painful and exquisite:

Fortunately there were, I admit, exceptions to all these things mostly when you suffered in silence, and affection and kindliness by their own strength overcame all obstacles, and moved me immediately. Admittedly this was rare, but it was wonderful. For instance, when in earlier times, in hot summers, when you were tired after lunch, I saw you having a nap at the office, your elbow on the desk; or when you joined us in the country, in the summer holidays, on Sundays, worn out from work at the office; or the time when Mother was gravely ill and you stood holding on to the bookcase, shaking with sobs; or when, during my last illness, you came tiptoeing to Ottla's* room to see me, stopping in the doorway, craning your neck to see me, and out of consideration for me only waved your hand to me. At such times one would lie back and weep for happiness, and one weeps again now, writing it down. You have a

_____

* One of Franz's sisters.

particularly beautiful, very rare way of quietly, contentedly, approvingly smiling ... (*DF*, 155).

Wondrous moments that Kafka did not forget; but neither did he fail to realize that they had had, by contrast, only one other result: to render his suffering more vivid, to increase his "sense of guilt" and to make the world for him "still more incomprehensible" (*DF*, 155).

... In all my thinking I was, after all, under the heavy pressure of your personality, even in that part of it—and particularly in that—which was not in accord with yours. All these thoughts, seemingly independent of yours, were from the beginning loaded with the burden of your harsh and dogmatic judgments ... (*DF*, 145).

Such is the balance sheet of the perverse upbringing that Franz Kafka was subjected to. It may even be called a model upbringing in reverse. Franz summed up in a word its result when he concluded his long letter: "Not even your mistrust of yours, after all, is as great as my self-mistrust, which you inculcated in me" (*DF*, 196). It is from this point in the relationship with his father that the black sun* shines tragically, obstinately, on all aspects of Kafka's life:

Marrying is barred to me through the fact that it is precisely and peculiarly your most intimate domain (*DF*, 191).

... Since nothing was in my very own, undoubted, sole possession, determined unequivocally only by me—in sober truth a disinherited son—naturally even the thing nearest at hand, my own body, became insecure (*DF*, 178).

... I was given the liberty to choose my career. But was I still at all capable of really making use of such liberty? Had I still my confidence in my own capacity to achieve a real career? (*DF*, 179).
I could not but side with the staff [at his father's store] (*DF*, 162).
I found equally little means of escape from you in Judaism (*DF*, 171).

* An allusion to the "black sun of Melancholy" from Gérard de Nerval's *El Desdichado*—"... et mon luth constellé/Porte le *soleil noir* de la *Mélancolie*"—which in turn was inspired by Albrecht Dürer's engraving *Melancholia* in which strong rays of sunlight beat down upon the contemplative allegorical figure of Melancholy [trans. note].

My writing was all about you; all I did there, after all, was to bemoan what I could not bemoan upon your breast (*DF*, 177).

On every side, Kafka came up against the prodigious specter of his father, a dark Proteus blocking all exits. In the face of such a presence, there was no other means of revolt and salvation except flight. That is the way out that Kafka finally took when he left for Berlin with Dora Dymant in 1923. By then it was too late.

Oedipus complex? No doubt. But, let us please avoid reducing the numberless varied experiences of Oedipus' tragedy to mechanical variants of an explanatory gimmick that is never any more than the beginning of an explanation. For the further one goes the more one sees that one is entering into a labyrinth of explanations. The more light is shed into the wings offstage, the more wings one discovers, deeper, ever more numerous, more mysterious still than one had begun to suspect. The true power of psychoanalysis is that it explains the myth a good deal less by way of the complex than the complex by way of the myth; the very nature of myth is to be inexhaustible and fathomless.

This too Kafka was aware of. He had Freud in mind when he wrote *The Judgment*, but he objected to the claims of psychoanalysts of having arrived at definitive explanations. Kafka knew how to probe ever deeper and further. "The revolt of the son against the father," he said one day to Janouch, "is one of the primeval themes of literature . . ." It is a tragedy, or rather a comedy, Franz added with bitter irony, and in support he cited Synge's play *The Playboy of the Western World*, in which a rebellious son brags of having bludgeoned his father, but who then finds himself embarrassed and reduced to an untenable situation by the reappearance of the "old man." "I see you are very skeptical," exclaimed Janouch. ". . . This struggle is usually only shadow boxing," Franz replied. "Age is the future of youth, which sooner or later it must reach. So why struggle? To become old sooner? For a quicker departure?" (*CWK*, 41–42). By which we may understand: The struggle is real enough, but its result is ephemeral, therefore without real substance. Why struggle, since death in any case comes to end everything? There all human combat finally fails. But the very nature of youth and of adulthood is precisely to make of death an "abstraction," to struggle and to live as though death did not exist.

This idea expressed to Janouch sums up the defeat of Franz, crushed by the destructive tyranny of his father, and devoted, like the son in *The Judgment*, to making of his existence nothing more than a multiform and prolonged suicide, but a suicide all the same.

The unbreathable atmosphere of Kafka's tales is not, then, a gratuitous invention of his imagination; his art flows out of the conflict with his father, it manifests that conflict and re-creates it all over again. In the letter to his father he wrote:

You struck nearer home with your dislike of my writing and all that, unknown to you, was connected with it. Here I had, in fact, got some distance away from you by my own efforts, even if it was slightly reminiscent of the worm that, as a foot tramples on the tail end of it, breaks loose with its top end and drags itself aside. To a certain extent I was in safety; there was a chance to breathe freely (*DF*, 176).

Art here reflects the positive phase of the force of reaction. The attempt to escape beyond the paternal sphere appears then as a valid and even successful attempt. But this is only the initial phase, for there is the inevitable shock of the counter-reaction:

My vanity and my ambition did suffer, it is true, under your soon proverbial way of hailing the arrival of my books: "Put it on my bedside table!" (as it happened, you were usually playing cards when a book came) ... (*DF*, 176–77).

As in every dialogue, communication between father and son could have taken two paths: the short path of the spoken word or the long path of the written word. Between Hermann and Franz the short path was cut off. The long path seems to have been cut off as well, since father and son lived nearly always with one another and since Franz tried only once, at the age of

thirty-six, to write that finally free and open letter, which is all
the more interminable for having been interminably postponed.
But in the final analysis it was a message that could not be de-
livered to its intended recipient, for in actuality Franz dared
only give it to his mother, and she in turn did not dare to trans-
mit it to her husband. As in *The Castle*, women have the power
of intercession, but it is a power so limited as to be practically
useless.

Thus there remained for Franz only one desperate possibility
of hope: to take a path parallel to the long path by substituting
for the outright letter, addressed to his father designated by
name, a cryptographic message woven into symbolic fictions
charged with allusions and addressed as though to someone offstage. Was this not the logical extension of the manner in which
the father spoke of his son in the third person, addressing the
mother in the son's presence? But this path too had already been
tried and Franz knew the result. In 1913 and 1916 he had published *The Judgment* and *Metamorphosis*, which seem to us as
atrociously clear as they did to him, but the long path and veiled
language could not succeed any better than other methods in
reestablishing communication between father and son, for every
attempt ended at the closed gate to the short path, crushed by
that abrupt exclamation: "Put it on my bedside table!"

Needless to say, in spite of Franz's humble remark, all of this
infinitely surpasses the minor matter of a wound to his literary
vanity, for Hermann's taste was truly devoid of importance.
What Franz resented so frightfully was that not even affected
or willful disdain with regard to his most profound drama.

Suffering is all the more keen when there is no way out, no
recourse. Far from being alone in his attitude, the father could
assert that the whole family circle joined him in it. One Sunday
when the family was gathered at Kafka's grandparents' home,
enjoying an afternoon snack, Franz noted on a scrap of paper,
not without some spirit of provocation, several impressions for
a future novel:

An uncle who liked to make fun of people finally took the page that I was holding only weakly, looked at it briefly, handed it back to me, even without laughing, and only said to the others who were following him with their eyes, "The usual stuff," to me he said nothing (DI, 44).

Of course, Hermann might well have added, "My dear son can only write grotesque and absurd things without the slightest relation to the solidly real and affectionate life that we all lead." But how can we reproach Hermann when even today writers who have at their fingertips all the evidence still affirm seriously that all of Kafka's writings are unreal, phantasmagoric, and barren of significance.

Franz, however, categorically stated his case in that same letter to his father:

My writing was all about you; all I did there, after all, was to bemoan what I could not bemoan upon your breast. It was an intentionally long-drawn-out leave-taking from you, only although it was brought about by force on your part, it did not take its course in the direction determined by me (DF, 177).

If Kafka's short stories and novels are reread in the light of this perspective, one will see that apart from many other significant aspects, they conceal within them first of all a significant familial and more especially, a paternal orientation that is central to them. In certain of these tales, it is baldly apparent, notably in The Judgment. The same can be said for the story of Odradek, which bears the title "The Cares of a Family Man."*

The meaning of The Metamorphosis must also be reconsidered in this light. Is it not from one end to the other the story of a young man whose mysterious illness results in a change in him that renders him incapable of a normal life and unrecognizable to his own loved ones? The "bizarre" aspect of Gregor Samsa's case is clarified by converging rays of light: in addition to foreshadowing Kafka's tuberculosis, it symbolizes the monstrous familial peculiarity of Kafka's genius.

* The Penal Colony, (New York: Schocken, 1961), pp. 160–61.

In *Amerika*, the conflict with the father is found again as the origin of the hero's misfortunes, since it is this conflict (the result of a fault stemming from a pathological infantilism for which young Karl is hardly responsible) that determines Karl's exile to America. Moreover, as soon as he is in the New World, Karl finds once more the father as persecutor in the figures of his uncle and the Head Porter of the hotel who harass him for his illusory faults. As for the cook, as well as for the innkeeper's wife in *The Castle*, are they not shadows of the mother—devoted, compassionate, but powerless before the autocratic sovereignty of the father?

How can one not be aware, finally, of all the emanations of that terrible paternal influence in the figures of the Emperor in *The Great Wall of China*, of the former commandant in *The Penal Colony*, and of the civil servants in *The Castle* and *The Trial?* Are not the inaccessibility in which they all entrench themselves, the impossibility of truly communicating with them an exact reflection of Franz's situation with regard to Hermann?

There, in brief, are the books that Kafka's father had placed on his bedside table in order not to have his card game interrupted. But we have only begun.

2

The Elusive Bride

... We being what we are, marrying is barred to me through the fact that it is precisely and peculiarly your most intimate domain (*DF*, 191).

A peremptory statement indeed, but such an astonishing one that one may wonder if Franz might not have been delirious when he wrote it. In one sense he was delirious; there was no logical reason for the father's marriage to have stood in the way of the son's. But the difference between Kafka and all of us does not lie in the fact that Kafka alone is delirious while we are imperturbably sound of mind. The only certain difference is that Kafka was conscious of his delirium. Consciousness of it, however, did not suffice to cure him of it. For it is a fact that Kafka failed to overcome the mysterious obstacle that stood in the way of his marrying.

We have noted in fact his series of repeated failures with Felicia B., Julie Wohryzek, and Milena Jesenská. Must we attribute this series of failures to frivolity and lack of love? Certainly not. One has only to plunge into the diaries to sense how great was the thirst for love that devoured Franz. Even if one doubted it, given the strangeness of his reticences, how can one not shudder at an outcry such as the one he addressed to Felicia:

You belong to me, I have made you mine. I can't believe that there
was ever a woman in a fairy tale fought for harder and more des-
perately than I have fought for you within myself . . . (DII, 168).

Everything is revealed in this statement: the intensity of desire and the obstacle that stood between Kafka and the woman
he loved; not a social barrier, nor opposition from his family,
but a barrier within the very being of Franz Kafka. He is not
being either grandiloquent or "literary" when he compares that
struggle to those of fairy tale lovers. This statement is lucidity
itself, for he could not have better stated that he fought monsters
and chimeras of the worst sort, those born of the kingdom of
shadowy subjectivity whose tentacles reach out and grasp at the
heart of objective life. Brod was a witness to this mixture of
love and inhibition, as he shows when he writes: ". . . When a
letter came from F., he [Kafka] wouldn't eat for half a day, and
didn't open the letter" (FK, 164).

Kafka's love for Milena was no less torn. This is revealed in
his remarkable correspondence with her, remarkable because its
tone is unique—unique precisely because it is neither a correspondence of friendship nor of love in the usual sense of the
words, but the mutual discussion of a passionate heartbreak.
What are letters? To Milena, Franz declared that letter writing
"is, in fact, an intercourse with ghosts, and not only with the
ghost of the recipient but also with one's own ghost," and "a
terrible disintegration of souls."*

There will be those who will not fail immediately to seek out
some sexual anomaly here. Kafka himself declared that as a
young boy he was as little interested in sex as he was in the
Theory of Relativity (DII, 227). Concerning the cessation of
this lethargy, which corresponds to the age of Sleeping Beauty's
Castle,** we have two confirmations, one of them from Brod,

---

* Letters to Milena, trans. Tania & James Stern (New York: Schocken,
1962), p. 229.
** ". . . qui correspond à l'âge du château de la Belle au bois dormant
. . ." Charles Perrault's La Belle au bois dormant (Sleeping Beauty) can of
course be interpreted as an allegory of postponed sexual awakening, but
M. Carrouges' reference to the castle's age is obscure [trans. note].

according to whom Franz's sexual awakening was associated with a "French governess or some Frenchwoman" (*FK*, 9), the other from Franz himself, when he relates that his initiation was the work of comrades, that he reproached his father for not having informed him about sexual matters, and that the latter immediately replied with brutal hygienic advice. This sort of occurrence is banal enough not to have marked Franz any more than many other boys. Yet, Franz reacted to it with unheard of violence: "In keeping with your nature you took it quite simply, only saying something to the effect that you could give me some advice about how I could go in for these things without danger." Franz does not state what this advice was, but it would not be surprising if it were that of having recourse only to "professionals," with the customary precautions of course (Franz was sixteen at the time).

... What you were advising me to do was, after all, in your opinion and, still far more, in my opinion at that time, the filthiest thing possible. The fact that you were prepared to see to it that physically speaking I should not bring any of the filth home with me was incidental, for in that way you were only protecting yourself, your own household. The main thing was, rather, that you remained outside your own advice, a married man, a pure man, exalted above these things; this was intensified for me at that time probably even more through the fact that marriage too seemed to me to be shameless and hence it was impossible for me to refer the general information I had picked up about marriage to my parents. In this way you became still more pure, rose still higher. The thought that you might perhaps have given yourself similar advice too before marriage was to me utterly unthinkable. So there was almost no smudge of earthly filth on you at all. And precisely you were pushing me, just as though I were predestined to it, down into this filth, with a few frank words. And so if the world consisted only of me and you, a notion I was much inclined to have, then this purity of the world came to an end with you and, by virtue of your advice, the filth began with me. In itself it was, of course, incomprehensible that you should thus condemn me; only old guilt and profoundest contempt of your side could explain it to me. And so this again was something that struck home to my innermost being, and very hard too (*DF*, 185, 186).

This passage is obviously of capital importance. It would be worthwhile to analyze it at length in the light of general views with regard to initiation to the sexual act. It stresses very well the way in which puritanism and libertinism have associated in order to disfigure the Judeo-Christian view of marriage as a continuation of the flow of the river of life that began with Genesis.

Many people view marital or extramarital sexuality indiscriminately as a quagmire to which, however, one can accommodate oneself by the application of a little down-to-earth wisdom. Franz on the contrary was at the age of absolutes; indeed, he lived always on that plane, and he never agreed to live deliberately according to any such double standard of values. But crushed by the family Manicheanism, he assigned to his father the pure side of marriage and relegated himself to that side of it which was at once shameful and impossible.

This kind of explanation, of course, cannot exhaust the mystery of human behavior—that of Franz less than any other—but it does help one to understand how Max Brod could have preserved the memory of Franz's confidences as revealing "a certain temporary mistrust" of the sexual act (FK, 37) and "unsatisfied feelings as far as the world of women is concerned" (FK, 117).

One can guess how painful all this must have been for Franz. Yet it is not certain that just how far the cruelty of that suffering went has been fully understood. If one merely glances rapidly over the long series of Kafka's loves, including his brief encounters with prostitutes, one might imagine that his life was one of debauchery and that this was in truth the obstacle to his marrying. It is undoubtedly true that he had a great number of amorous "adventures," but his confidences concerning them are filled with an uneasiness and ambiguity that is far removed from libertinism.

On July 3, 1916, his thirty-third birthday, he noted: "First day in Marienbad with F. Door to door, keys on either side" (DII, 156). Not a word further. Three days later he added: "I have never yet been intimate with a woman apart from that time in Zuckmantel. And then again with the Swiss girl in Riva. The first was a woman, and I was ignorant; the second a child, and I was utterly confused" (*DII*, 159).

With regard to prostitutes there is no less ambiguity. Sometimes, as on at least one occasion during a visit to a Parisian brothel, Kafka fled in disarray. Brod is the only one who relates that Kafka had a "passion" for a barmaid named Hansi who made him very unhappy: "You can see that, too, in a photograph taken of him together with Hansi, but in which he looks as if he would like to run away the next moment" (*FK*, 116).

Kafka's most characteristic admission is perhaps this note made in 1913:

I intentionally walk through the streets where there are whores. Walking past them excites me, the remote but nevertheless existent possibility of going with one. Is that grossness? But I know no better, and doing this seems basically innocent to me and causes me almost no regret" (*DI*, 309).

Several years later he was to say to Janouch:

The term "will o' the wisp" (bludčika) for this kind of women is wonderfully true. How wretched, abandoned, frozen men must be, when they wish to warm themselves by these marsh gases! (*CWK*, 104).

With venereal pleasures, as with love and marriage, there is always the same painful drama of desire, attempted contact and, finally, flight. Kafka's painful indecision is projected into the strange episode that causes Karl's departure in *Amerika*: the young man lets himself be seduced by his parents' maid without even understanding the nature of what is happening. Taking part in the seduction almost out of indifference, he is acted upon by the woman, so to speak. Even K., in a libertinish episode in *The Castle*, shows a strange boredom and passivity.

On what seems to be the opposite side of the coin, Joseph K. in *The Trial* poses as an egregious libertine and is ostensibly disdainful of the details of his case. He takes no interest, for exam-

ple, in the conference to plan his defense that takes place in his
lawyer's home, and he leaves to pay court to the maid in the
corridors or in the kitchen. Even in the anteroom of the courtroom, he pursues his amorous exploits while the bailiff and his
wife drag their bed into the room.

The same sort of ostentation, in general, is found in *The Castle*
in the scene where K. moves his and Frieda's bed right into the
classroom, or where he rolls about with her under the counter
of the hotel, which nonetheless is assigned to the fearsome func-
tionaries from the Castle. Similar provocative scenes can also
be found in *Amerika*, on the occasion of meetings between Karl
and Clara or Brunelda.

This spectacular invasion of beds in the most incongruous
places has nothing to do with the so-called unreality that some
critics gratuitously attribute to Kafka. It has a truly erotic sense:
it is the immediate objectivization of the incongruous thoughts
that haunted Kafka, with disregard for the usual functional
compartmentalizing of thought.

At the office one day, for example, he stopped short in the
process of dictating a report and could do nothing but contemplate the typist. In one swift moment, he realized that his life
was bogged down in just such red tape as this. The violent wind
of poetry was there, jostling everything, but Franz alone entered
into that "other" state of perception; everyone around him
remained clinging to "reality" (*DI*, 76–77).

He felt that same fascination on another occasion: while
sitting in a lawyer's office, listening as the lawyer read aloud
an agreement in which there was a question of his possible future
wife and children, Kafka was "confounded" by the typist.
Though a lawyer himself, he heard not another word of the
contract being read: "I saw across the table from me a table with
two large chairs and a smaller one around it. At the thought that
I should never be in a position to seat in these or any other three
chairs myself, my wife and my child, there came over me a
yearning for this happiness . . ." (*DI*, 141).

In this light, the appearance of beds and of amorous revels

in the classroom or in courthouses is not debauchery, but rather suggests the fictitious victory of love in the very places that deny it, places that oppressed Kafka. This, however, does not exclude the necessity of taking into account, on the same level, an entirely different perspective on the matter.

We have seen, in fact, that the strange feeling of innocence and guilt that cannot be dissociated in K. is clearly explained from the moment one recognizes it as a transposition of the drama that occurred between Felicia and Kafka, including the very precise relationship between the parody of justice in the unkempt "courtroom" in *The Trial* and the parody of a trial suggested in the meeting at the hotel in Berlin between Kafka and Felicia's parents (*DII*, 65–66). Far from being gratuitous and isolated, such analogies are only the first, most obvious points in an immense network of concordances and allusions of every kind.

"Kafka read the first chapter of *The Trial* to Brod less than two months after his first break with Felicia. Joseph K. was thirty years old when he was arrested, and he was executed on the eve of his thirty-first birthday. From the first lines, the initial K. indicates to the reader that it is Kafka who is the accused, but a policeman's first name, Franz, suggests that it is also Kafka who carries out the arrest. If Joseph K. is innocent when he is arrested, Kafka at that moment already considered himself sufficiently guilty so that in the space of one year that the trial requires—trials of this kind supposedly require several years—Joseph K. becomes in his turn sufficiently guilty to merit execution. Moreover, Joseph K. becomes guilty in a little less than three weeks; at this point the forces of justice, in view of their curious delay in carrying out the sentence, seem to want to allow him to rectify the crimes that he, on the other hand, wishes merely to multiply." We have taken the foregoing remarks from an excellent article by Michel Cournot,* who cites as evidence the astonishing cascade of frivolous acts, impudences, and provocations that follow one another in Joseph K.'s

* *L'Arche*, No. 23.

behavior and that, having nothing to do with his legal guilt, betray all kinds of anguish, inclination towards scandalous behavior, and reasons for scruples. Thus Joseph K. embraces Mlle. B. by force, he insults the Inspector who comes to arrest him, he refuses to allow himself to be questioned by the Examining Magistrate, and he flees from the courtroom. While on the other hand, he treats both Mlle. Bürstner and Mlle. Mortag in a cavalier manner; he dismisses his lawyer in order to replace him with a supposedly influential painter. "Finally, caught between his bank and his trial, as Kafka was caught between his insurance company and literature, Joseph K. also becomes guilty in the eyes of the bank by arriving late, by refusing to accept the invitation of the Assistant Manager, then by multiplying his absences, by leaving work early, by his negligence, and by his becoming generally useless to the bank—the last fact seeming to intervene in the final outcome" (*Ibid.*).

As Michel Cournot further points out, the three major aspects of the novel—the trial, the women, and the bank—are intermingled ceaselessly throughout: "It is because he has been arrested that Joseph K. for the first time enters Mlle. Bürstner's room where, moreover, three bank employees are waiting for him. That evening he asks Mlle. Bürstner's aid in his trial; he then refuses the invitation of the Assistant Manager of the bank in order to answer the summons of the Examining Magistrate, and on his way to the court session he passes the bank employees in the street," etc.

Kafka's very life and its interrelationships with the novel explain very well the principle of these "oddities": "Thus, what seemed haphazard and fantastic becomes perfectly justifiable. It is not strange that Joseph K. discovers the executioner flogging the warders in a storeroom of the bank, since the marriage with F. (represented by justice) deprived Kafka of all hope of quitting his job (represented by the bank); it is not strange that K. meets Mlle. Bürstner the evening of his execution and that he himself conducts his executioners to the place of his death by following the young woman, since Kafka wished to atone for the fault committed against F. (represented by Mlle. Bürstner). As a last example, the reader should now no longer be surprised that Joseph K., opening the Examining Magistrate's notebook, reads therein not an article from the legal code (which would destroy the parable), but this entry: *How Grete Was Plagued by Her Husband Hans"* (*Ibid.*).

In *The Trial* one finds the dark pyramid of involved trials that Kafka instigated in secret: First, the trial of the son, Joseph K., by the father, hidden behind the labyrinthian processes of justice, for the son's crime is that of not having had the strength to love his fiancée to the point of accepting marriage; and only the father, not ordinary justice, could take it upon himself to reproach the son for it. Next, the same trial turns against the father, for it is the overwhelming image of the father that saps the strength of the son and deprives him of the courage to marry. This is doubly manifest in the miserable familial setting of the courtroom in *The Trial* and in the way in which the son flouts the father's power manifested in the job that he imposes on the son (the bank, the image of the insurance office) and behind the tyranny of justice (the image of the familial, social, and religious demands inculcated by the father). Finally, it is also the trial of the son by the son, since Franz delights in emphasizing the gratuitous provocations of Joseph K., his useless acts of rebellion, and ultimately his willing acceptance of condemnation and death.

In *The Penal Colony*, the two themes of suicide at the father's command (*The Judgment*) and legal execution (*The Trial*) are fused into a single act of sacrificial suicide through voluntary substitution for a condemned man on the torture machine. This is the most terrifying myth that Kafka created. Here one finds the traits of the father in the former commandant and those of the son in the person of the officer–victim. But it is not only a myth of terror, for the torture machine evokes directly the sexual process as the black and mechanical process of self-

destruction, the myth of the "bachelor machine" in which all
Kafka's suffering and anguish find their culmination.* There
can be no more tragic illustration of his famous aphorism:

Celibacy and suicide are on similar levels of understanding, suicide
and a martyr's death not so by any means, perhaps marriage and a
martyr's death (*DF*, 77).

The relationship that he introduces then between celibacy and
suicide, marriage and martyrdom, is the equation of facts for
which he could find no solution. Between celibacy and marriage
he did not cease to wander along a perpetually oscillating trajectory of unstable love affairs.

Therein lies the principal factor behind his tragic odyssey
of love. For in spite of what he had said in the letter to his father
about the shame of marriage, in spite of the vacillations in his
sexual and love life, he admired marriage as the highest of
possible human realities:

Marrying, founding a family, accepting all the children that come,
supporting them in this insecure world and even guiding them a
little as well, is, I am convinced, the utmost a human being can
succeed in doing at all (*DF*, 183).

---

* It is impossible here to go into the long analysis that I devoted to this
aspect of Kafka's life and work in the special study entitled *Les Machines
célibataires* (The Bachelor Machines), based on a detailed confrontation
between Kafka's network of symbols and that of Marcel Duchamp's famous *Large Glass* (*La Mariée mise à nue par ses célibataires*). While waiting to take advantage, in a new edition of my study, of several interesting
remarks contained in M. Mayoux's article (*Bizarre*, Nos. I and II), I
should like to express my deepest thanks to those who were kind enough
to encourage me in its undertaking, particularly Marcel Duchamp, whose
personal letters at the time brought me expressions of the highest esteem
I could ever have hoped for.

[M. Carrouge's study, *Les Machines célibataires* (Paris: Arcanes, 1954),
is now out of print but is currently being translated into English for publication in Great Britain by the house of Jonathan Cape. For a detailed
discussion of Duchamp's *Large Glass* and its symbolic implications, which
includes several brief references to M. Carrouge's 1954 study, see: Robert
Ledel, *Marcel Duchamp* (New York: Grove Press, 1959), pp. 30–33; 70–
73 (trans. note).]

Further on he insists once again:

Marriage is certainly the pledge of the most acute form of self-liberation and independence. I should have a family, the highest thing that one can achieve, in my opinion, and so too the highest thing you have achieved; I should be your equal . . . (*DF*, 190).

Here Kafka makes us feel the heart of the tragedy. In his mercurial, unstable, or simply inconclusive love affairs, he remains in an adolescent state. In order to overthrow the power of the paternal image, he had to substitute his own image for his father's and become himself the father of a new family. Equality thus conquered is not static, it parallels the mythical act of dethroning the father. Long before the tragedy of Oedipus, that of the genealogy of the gods in the bloody succession of Uranos, Kronos, and Zeus (Uranus, Saturnus, and Jupiter) is the mirror-image of consanguinary descent and of the conflict between human generations. This myth embodies the non-pathological necessity of Oedipus' "complex." Created by the father, the son remains rebellious and unsatisfied until he becomes a creator in his turn. The bachelor is the orphan of the future. It is only when he has become in his turn a husband and father that the son definitively resolves the conflict with his father. Thus, it is not by chance that, in the legend, Kronos cuts off the testicles of his father, Uranos, and that Kronos in turn devours his children (with the exception of Zeus who escapes from him) because he sees in them rivals who will overthrow him. These acts are the barbaric expression of the conflict between generations, but they embody the truth of that conflict.

But since Kafka knew this so well, since he had such a thirst for liberating love, why should his repeated attempts at marriage have come to naught? Because of the paternal obsession, Franz tells us. But why did that obsession produce the effect that it did?

Here again we must refer to the very image that Franz drew of his father in order to grasp the external cause of his inhibition:

The most important obstacle to marriage . . . is the no longer eradicable conviction that what is essential to supporting a family and, more, to guiding it is what I have recognized in you, and indeed everything rolled into one, good and bad, as it is organically combined in you . . . (DF, 192–93).

This is the external obstacle, but it is not the only one, and one must search in more secret areas to bring to light the forces that prevented him from surmounting it. He repeats in another passage:

The essential obstacle . . . was that I am obviously intellectually incapable of marriage. This manifests itself in the fact that from the moment when I make up my mind to marry I can no longer sleep, my head burns day and night, life can no longer be called life, I stagger about in despair. It is not actually worries that bring this about . . . they are like worms completing the work on the corpse, but the decisive blow comes from elsewhere. It is the general pressure of anxiety, of weakness, of self-contempt (DF, 189–90).

In fact, Kafka was to some extent right in not admitting to what he humorously calls "the good and bad" qualities of his father, but they were not indispensable for raising a family. A lawyer, a professional man, Franz had no serious social reason for thinking himself incapable of supporting a family. Behind the veil of this false reason, the true motive for Franz's desperate doubts was the effect of the irreparable damage done by the father's tyranny during the son's youth.

As comprehensible as the working of that kind of fatality inherent in Kafka's destiny may be, it remains nonetheless mysterious. Paternal tyranny does not always have such a mechanically crushing effect. Most sons so tyrannized steel themselves as long as needs be and eventually leave home in order to build their lives in their own way. Others rebel by attempting to do everything contrary to what their fathers did. Others, weaker, remain submissive and broken, incapable of breaking out of the shell of paternal influence and founding their own independence. Must Kafka, then, be placed in the last category?

There was indeed something of the broken man in Kafka;

however, he maintained an incredible patience in his love and respect for that tyrannical father. But that was not the vice that paralyzed him, for that love and respect had nothing in common with servile obedience and spiritless submission. Franz was lucid, and that lucidity itself was a form of defiance that he put into action not only through his occasional provocations, but especially through the continual provocation that was inherent in his literary activity.

Broken, Kafka remained undefeated. Neither submissive nor rebellious in the usual senses of these words, he was the incarnation of the quiet rebel. At the beginning, torn apart and shoved by his father into the phantasmagorically real world of his inner consciousness, he was beyond his father's reach, but not beyond the consequences that he himself willed, for he continued to tear himself apart.

When he says that the highest happiness is marriage, with the same voice he declares immediately that he is intellectually incapable of marriage. He went so far as to explain this more precisely:

I do not envy particular married couples, I simply envy all married couples together . . . the happiness of married life in general . . . [but] the happiness to be found in any one marriage, even in the likeliest case, would probably plunge me into despair (*DII*, 194–95).

Within Franz himself there were two men who struggled continually against one another. The one said:

The infinite, deep, warm, saving happiness of sitting beside the cradle of one's child opposite its mother (*DII*, 204).

The other said (this statement was made in 1913):

Coitus as punishment for the happiness of being together. Live as ascetically as possible, more ascetically than a bachelor, that is the only way for me to endure marriage. But she? (*DI*, 296).

And yet again:

Sensual love deceives one as to the nature of heavenly love; it could not do so alone, but since it unconsciously has the element of heavenly love within it, it can do so (*DF*, 42).

If Kafka never abandoned the idea that marriage represented the highest possible form of happiness, this thought never succeeded in destroying in him the inveterate feeling that there was something "shameful" in marriage, as he expressed it in the letter to his father.

In addition to Kafka's ambiguous behavior in sexual matters and his relations with his family, one must also consider his problems with regard to marriage from a biological point of view:

. . . I am descended from my parents, am linked to them and my sisters by blood . . . at bottom [I] have more respect for it than I realize. Sometimes this bond of blood too is the target of my hatred; the sight of the double bed at home, the used sheets, the nightshirts carefully laid out, can exasperate me to the point of nausea, can turn me inside out;* it is as if I had not been definitively born, were continually born anew into the world out of the stale life in that stale room . . . were indissolubly joined with all that loathsomeness, in part even if not entirely, at least it still clogs my feet which want to run, they are still stuck fast in the original shapeless pulp (*DII*, 167).

This passage is a key one; it signifies beyond any doubt a horror of the sexual act and of the bourgeois ritual, but more profoundly still, a horror of the biological fact of being born of flesh.

It is important to note here that, contrary to the old puritanical tradition and contrary to the atheistic tradition that keeps this puritanical tradition alive detesting it with good reason, this horror of the flesh is in no way Judaic in origin: God created the flesh and willed that man and woman "shall be one flesh" (Genesis 2:24). This horror is no less opposed to the Christian tradition, which has never considered the sexual union in marriage as shameful, but rather as sacred. This by no means in any way obviates whatever Saint Paul may have said about the "weakness of the flesh," which speaks of the sexual act in another and contrary sense that in no way contradicts the sacred

* This theme seems to amount almost to a fixation with Kafka. He evokes it in 1913 (*DI*, 292) as well as in the above entry of 1916.

nature of the marital union. Indeed, the fundamental principles
of Christianity are expressed in terms of divine materialism:
"The Word was made flesh"; "My flesh is food indeed" (John
6:56,57)* "I believe in the resurrection of the body." No other
philosophy or religion has rendered the flesh divine in the way
Christianity has. In fact, condemnation of the body and of the
flesh is typically Manichean, Buddhist, Platonic.

However, while some spiritualistic mystics from time to time
come to forget their corporeal reality to the point of thinking
themselves entirely happy and "liberated" from the body, Kafka
did not forget it. It is in this that he remains admirably and
painfully human. Torn between the two aspects of human
nature, he knew that he was torn. The two parts of himself,
having become strangers to one another, felt themselves mutually estranged. His external self, crushed and rejected, came
to appear to him as a disorbited and uncontrollable part of
himself, while his inner life became incommensurate, unfathomable, prodigiously expanded and open upon every kind of abyss.
This dissociation was carried over into various other aspects of
his life.** In the same way that he was torn between his true
spiritual self and his corporeal self, he was torn between his
true vocation, literature, and his carnal profession, the insurance
business; between ideal love and carnal love: he projected into
the women he loved the same dualism that he found in himself.

For Kafka love retained its full materialistic value at the same
time that it held something of the miraculous. It had thereby the
capacity of forcibly breaking down obstacles to communication.
Whatever devastation the father had wreaked within the son's
being, the woman was in a unique position of maintaining a
power greater than the father's and was thus able to render to

* In the translation from the Latin Vulgate version of *The New Testa-*
ment (Paterson, N. J.: St. Anthony Guild Press, 1941).

** For a significant impression of *dédoublement*, see *DI*, pp. 74, 105.
[*N.B.* The term *dédoublement* in French refers to the phenomenon, often
vividly hallucinatory, of a person's being aware of the presence of another
"self" acting independently of one's normal, accustomed self (trans.
note).]

the son the thirst for love and life. Franz knew that this power
exists, he admired it, he savored it with exaltation. Yet this power
is not limitless, for the son finally finds himself in connivance
with the father. Exiled by the father into a phantasmagoric
world, the son takes that world for his own. Reduced to a sub-
stanceless state, he comes to prefer his phantasmagoric existence
and transforms every woman he approaches into a phantom. He
does not communicate with her "in body and in soul." In her and
in him everything is dislocated, and the phantoms endlessly
search for and elude each other like shadows in the Elysian
Fields.

Kafka was aware of this process. He knew Kierkegaard's
drama (*DI*, 298; *DII*, 164–65; 232), he depicted tragically the
bachelor's unhappiness, painfully weighed the reasons for and
against his marriage: "What I accomplished was only the result
of being alone," Kafka wrote, ". . . but I am incapable, alone, of
bearing the assault of my own life, the demands of my own
person, the attacks of time and old age, the vague pressure of
the desire to write, sleeplessness, the nearness of insanity . . .";
however, he also declared, ". . . It is even improbable that I know
how to live with anyone" (*DI*, 292).

He hesitated endlessly between the two sides of this dilemma,
forming, breaking, and reforming engagements only to break
them again. If he never succeeded in forming anything but, for
all practical purposes, broken engagements, it was because deep
within himself there was no real hesitation. He made only useless,
desperate efforts that were so deliberately ineffectual that nothing could be accomplished. It was always the desire for solitude
that carried the day. In the depth of his solitude he cohabited
with his phantoms, and not for anything in the world did he
wish to see a ray of light enter into the dark chamber where he
brought them to life:

I hate everything that does not relate to literature, conversations
bore me (even if they relate to literature), to visit people bores me,
the sorrows and joys of my relatives bore me to my soul. Conversations take the importance, the seriousness, the truth out of everything I think (*DI*, 292).

It was this that decided everything. To tie himself to another being, he felt, was like "passing into the other"; it meant "I'll never be alone again." It also meant becoming another man through the power of a woman, but "would it not be at the expense of my writing? Not that, not that!" And then too, his material and professional life was also involved in this opposition between love and writing: "Alone, I could perhaps some day really give up my job. Married, it will never be possible" (*DI*, 292–93).

As in Kafka's works, once again everything is interrelated: the specter of the father, the job, the woman, and the autonomous will of the hero. Underneath this apparent incoherence, Kafka saw only too clearly the hidden coherence. What in every case ties together the seemingly disparate elements of the phantasmagoria is the gordian knot of reality:

Hence it is a defensive instinct in me that won't tolerate my having the slightest degree of lasting ease and smashes the marriage bed, for example, even before it has been set up. (*DII*, 217).

. . . Everything in me revolted against [marriage], much as I always loved F. (*DII*, 24).

He refused to accept being helped by the woman he loved or being bound by her. He never ceased to think nostalgically of her, but he did not continue any less fiercely to penetrate ever farther into the depths of the wilderness of exile, freedom, terror, and the fantastic.

In the midst of the conflict that was tearing him apart, he emitted these searing words:

The wish for an unthinking, reckless solitude (*DI*, 288).
I'll shut myself off from everyone to the point of insensibility [my italics] (*DI*, 297).

Kafka was not speaking here of losing himself in sleep, but in the inexpressible, at the frontier of madness and of bitterest lucidity, in the loss of "normal" consciousness, the vertiginous fall into the black brilliance that bathed his own existence as it does the world of the phantoms to which he gave life with his own blood.

3

Physical Destruction

In *The Metamorphosis,* Gregor Samsa is in bed when he awakens transformed into a vermin. As bizarre as this misadventure is, Kafka tells it as naturally as he would have declared that Gregor had been stricken with smallpox or leprosy. Kafka saw no necessity for giving the least explanation—even an imaginary one—and the rest of the story unfolds in a logical, tragically simple manner.

Is Gregor Samsa's bed simply a sickbed? Beds in fact abound in Kafka's tales and if, in the preceding chapter they were found to have an erotic significance, another no less apparent significance must be acknowledged here. These beds are often sickbeds: that of the father in *The Judgment,* the lawyer in *The Trial,* the mayor and the innkeeper's wife in *The Castle,* the Emperor in *The Wall of China,* and, the ultimate example, the bed in which the doctor in *A Country Doctor* is forced to lie down beside his patient. In *The Hunter Gracchus* the bed takes the form of a bier, and in *The Penal Colony* it is actually an operating table where the condemned man is surgically treated, dissected, and put to death.

The extraordinary importance of sickness in Kafka's work is in a sense a test of its artistic stature. If the novel is an esthetic game for its author and an entertainment for its public, it goes without saying that sickbeds and the sufferings of their occupants amount merely to a romanesque theme. An exception to this rule can scarcely be found, except in a few powerfully realistic works, for sickness is the bitterest and the most sordid of concrete images of reality.

Thus we find another remarkable indication of Kafka's realism in that long row of beds that appears through his work. In them can be seen a new, intimate link between Kafka's writings and his life: these imaginary beds represent the presentiment if not the direct projection of Kafka's own bed in which he died gnawed by tuberculosis after having dragged on with the disease for years.

But to stop at such a simple interpretation would leave us far from the profound interrelationships that, as always with Kafka, are manifest in this image. The most striking of these interrelationships is summed up in the fact that in July, 1917 Kafka renewed his relationship with Felicia, only to break it off definitively the following December, after untold anguish. It was precisely during this period, in the month of August, that he first coughed up blood. A mere coincidence? Kafka pondered so searchingly over this incident that he wrote on September 15: "If the infection in your lungs is only a symbol, as you say, a symbol of the infection whose inflamation is called F. . . ." (*DII*, 182). He makes no affirmation here, but only poses a simple supposition. In truth, however, he was putting himself to the torture.

This declaration of Kafka has struck so many, that one has come to suppose that his tuberculosis, deriving in a purely mechanical way from his incapacity to marry, could ultimately be attributed to his "father complex." However, the agonizing question that Kafka was asking himself in this matter cannot be stricken from the record.

With the question of sexuality one must return to Kafka's expressed "horror of being born," that is, to the most elementary biological level. The theme of sickness leads us back again to the biological level and to a situation that existed long before the fruitless engagement intervened.

Once again Franz's diagnosis of the origin of his malady can be found in the letter to his father:

As far as I can think I have had such anxieties, of the very deepest kind about asserting my spiritual existence that everything else was a matter of indifference to me (*DF*, 178).

In reality he tried to erect a shell of indifference as "the sole defense against destruction of the child's nerves by fear and a sense of guilt" (*Ibid.*).

One always finds the same root at the origin of the destruction of Kafka's sense of vitality. He explained in detail how the process developed:

All that occupied my mind was worry about myself, and this in various ways. There was, for instance, the worry about my health; it began imperceptibly enough, with now and then a little anxiety about digestion, hair falling out, a spinal curvature, and so on, this intensifying in innumerable gradations, finally ending with a real illness . . . . Since nothing was in my very own undoubted, sole possession, determined unequivocally only by me—*in sober truth a disinherited son—naturally even the thing nearest at hand, my own body, became insecure* [my italics]; I shot up, tall and lanky, without knowing what to do with my lankiness, the burden being too heavy, the back becoming bent; I scarcely dared to move or, least of all, to do gymnastics and so I remained weakly: I was amazed by every-thing (that did not trouble me) as by a miracle, for instance my good digestion; that sufficed to make me lose it, and so now the way was open to every sort of hypochondria, until finally under the strain of the superhuman effort of wanting to marry . . . blood came from the lung (*DF*, 178–179).

The process of Kafka's self-destruction is there before our eyes. Its two aspects are on the one hand the affirmation of his spiritual existence placed above everything else, and on the other the irresistible feeling of anguish and guilt that led him to a feeling of insecurity about his own body. As the interior fire illuminated and broadened the spirit, the body was being gutted and ravaged. Before his father's assaults the son escaped through the subterranean passage of the spirit, but what was an act of self-defense was also suicidal, for the body could not follow the same path as the spirit. While the spirit fled into the distance, the body was being consumed. Under the influence of the doubly destructive blows of a faulty upbringing, this *dédoublement** ended in an exhausting struggle between the phantom and the man of flesh.

We have seen what repercussions that ruinous dissociation had in Kafka's love affairs. We must now examine the way in which it devoured him in his professional life. There also Kafka's life was divided in such a way that he was unable to impose any unity upon it. From one standpoint his daily job as bureaucrat, lawyer, and civil servant supported him and established his place in society. From another the only profession he wished to acknowledge was that of writer. But this was a nocturnal, unorganizable job, incapable of earning him a living, a "job" that filled his sleepless nights and even his holidays. These two professions represent yet two more aspects of himself that struggled against one another.

Again, hasty interpretations must be avoided. In the letter to his father, which dates from two years after the first coughing up of blood, Franz declared unequivocally that his illness was not the result of "excessive work" (*DF*, 179). As always, one must look deeper. Before his job, before his illness, and before his difficulties in love, one must seek out the same original source that lies in the initial rupture between the biological and the spiritual. Immediately after the remark quoted above Kafka added:

There were years in which, being in perfectly good health, I lazed away more time on the sofa than you in all your life, including all your illnesses . . . Probably I am constitutionally not lazy at all, but there was nothing for me to do. In the place where I lived I was spurned, condemned, fought to a standstill, and although I did make the utmost endeavors to escape to some other place, that was not work, for there it was a matter of something impossible, something that was, apart from small exceptions, unattainable for one of my resources.

*See trans. note, p. 47.

This then was the state in which I was given the liberty to choose my career. But was I still at all capable of really making use of such liberty? Had I still any confidence in my own capacity to achieve a real career? (*DF*, 179).

In reality there was only one true profession for Kafka, literature. He wanted neither journalism nor teaching, not to mention following his father's footsteps in the business world. As he was gnawed by self-doubt and deprived of all outside support, the freedom of choice that his father gave him was illusory and empty. It was thus that he drifted, through a time-honored procedure in Europe, into legal studies and the profession of civil servant.

Law school, he said, "told severely on my nerves . . . I was positively living, in an intellectual sense, on sawdust, which had, moreover, already been chewed for me in thousands of other peoples' mouths" (*DF*, 181).* He passed the examinations, however, and continued his studies as far as the doctorate. Then, after an obligatory service of one year in the civil and criminal courts, he worked for a year in an insurance company, the *Assicurazioni Generali*. He finally became an editor and technical writer in the semi-nationalized Workers' Insurance Institute in July, 1908. (He was not to leave this position until 1923, one year before his death.)

What could be more banal than this civil servant's career? It is of course customary, in distinguished literary criticism, to isolate hermetically the author's professional biography from his literary biography, as if the first were not worthy of mingling with the second. Unworthy perhaps, but the first is there. Was it not one and the same flesh and blood creature who practiced a profession that devoured him while providing him with a livelihood and who also created books that kept him alive while devouring him?

Kafka did do some writing at his office, but it was a superficial, functional kind of writing. Alone in his room he continued to write, but this was entirely different, a profound, deeply felt

---

* Cf. the felt gag in *The Penal Colony*.

kind of writing. Between the two there was a radical opposition: one was demanded by society, the other by solitude. Between the two there was a violent conflict, which is precisely why they were not isolated from one another by some kind of watertight door. The functional writing that he had to do at the office pursued him into his most secret defenses. In the relationships among Kafka's heroes, the law and legal problems occupy an immense place. This is most evident in *The Trial*, in *The Penal Colony*, and in *The Castle* in connection with the affair of the surveying contract.

In another writer the projection of law into literature would perhaps have produced only an "objective and realistic" depiction of human relationships seen from the legalistic angle, but in Kafka the degree of refraction in the treatment of these relationships is literally fantastic. As he himself failed to find a "viable profession," so the hero of *The Castle* fails to find a viable surveying contract. Where others succeed, Kafka, could not find success; too many obscure powers secretly opposed it. In the same way, *The Trial* comes to represent a monstrous legal proceeding in which we can see the reflection of all trials of inquisition, ancient or modern. But this novel is, first and foremost, Kafka's own personal drama; for up to the very moment of his death the legal code never ceased to persecute him—for no other reason than Kafka's own fatal decision to study law. Having imprudently poked his finger into the gears of the legal machinery, he ended being torn to shreds by it. Thus it is not by arbitrary chance that the executioner and the policemen are hidden in the storage room of the bank where Joseph K. works. Nor is it any more by chance that the letter of the law is graven into the flesh of the torture victim in the *Penal Colony*, and he is torn to shreds. This symbolic interpretation in no way excludes the other symbolic implications that are related to it, but it is the fundamental one. The machine is the work of the former commandant, a father figure. However, the officer, a son figure, asserts that he collaborated with the father in constructing the machine. It is entirely logical that the "machine" invented by the father should be the instrument of the son's death and that the son should use the machine to commit suicide as does the son in *The Judgment*. In his own life Franz carried out the same prolonged suicide with frightening calm all through the years between the time he received the Doctor of Laws degree and his death in the sanatorium in Kierling—not without the various fiancées having added additional needles to the machine.

One has only to read the *Diaries* to hear down through the years Franz's secret moans and to understand that, lacking powerful outside help from a woman, his situation was entirely hopeless:

The tremendous world I have in my head. But how free myself and free it without being torn to pieces. And a thousand times rather be torn to pieces than retain it in me or bury it. That, indeed, is why I am here, that is quite clear to me (*DI*, 288).

Rather than renounce his vocation, he preferred, while being fully aware of what was happening, to be torn apart. All during his life he was constantly aware of his situation and constantly reiterated his determination:

That I, so long as I am not freed of my office, am simply lost, that is clearer to me than anything else, it is just a matter, as long as it is possible, of holding my head so high that I do not drown (*DI*, 35).

This entry appears in 1910, when he had only just begun his life as a bureaucrat. The following year he wrote again:

When I wanted to get out of bed this morning I simply folded up. This has a very simple cause, I am completely overworked. Not by the office but by my other work. The office has an innocent share in it only to the extent that, if I did not have to go there, I could live calmly for my own work and should not have to waste these six hours a day which have tormented me to a degree that you cannot imagine, especially on Friday and Saturday because I was full of my own things . . . For me in particular it is a horrible double life from which there is probably no escape but insanity (*DI*, 44; see also *DI*, 61, 77).

In 1913, in the copy of a letter to Felicia's father, he wrote:

*My job is unbearable to me because it conflicts with my only desire
and my only calling, which is literature* [my italics]. Since I am
nothing but literature and can and want to be nothing else, my job
will never take possession of me, it may, however, shatter me completely, and this is by no means a remote possibility. Nervous states
of the worst sort control me without pause, and this year of worry
and torment about my and your daughter's future has revealed to
the full my inability to resist . . . And now compare me to your
daughter, this healthy, gay, natural, strong girl . . . She must be
unhappy with me (*DI*, 299).

Sapped by nervous exhaustion, Kafka was unable to find the
strength to join forces with the woman who loved him and
whom he loved and whose hand he saw held out to him from the
edge of the precipice. He was convinced that she could not save
him, that he could only drag her with him to perdition.

But we must turn once more to both the material and the
spiritual basis of the conflict in order to understand in what a
maelstrom Kafka's life-force was engulfed and swallowed up.
Nighttime played a dominant role in his life. First of all that
famous night whose extreme importance in the evolution of
Kafka's literary development we have already pointed out:

This story, *The Judgment*, I wrote at one sitting during the night
of the 22nd–23rd, from ten o'clock at night to six o'clock in the
morning. I was hardly able to pull my legs out from under the desk,
they had got so stiff from sitting. The fearful strain and joy, how
the story developed before me, as if I were advancing over water.
Several times during this night I heaved my own weight on my back
. . . How it turned blue outside the window. A wagon rolled by. Two
men walked across the bridge. At two I looked at the clock for the
last time. As the maid walked through the anteroom for the first
time I wrote the last sentence. Turning out the light and the light of
day. The slight pains around my heart. The weariness that disap-
peared in the middle of the night . . . Only *in this way* can writing
be done, only with such coherence, with such a complete opening
out of the body and the soul (*DI*, 275–76).

During such a night, weariness turns to exhaustion, but this
is immediately lightened by enthusiasm. If such a night is not
unique, it is most rare.

Kafka's diaries and personal notebooks are filled with extraordinarily numerous, intense, and precise accounts of dreams. These are not an indication that he slept deeply or a great deal. On the contrary, dreams of this nature occur only during brief, difficult, and interrupted sleep. On October 2, 1911 he wrote:

Sleepless night . . . I fall asleep soundly, but after an hour I wake up . . . And for the rest of the night, until about five, thus it remains, so that indeed I sleep but at the same time vivid dreams keep me awake. I sleep alongside myself, so to speak, while I myself must struggle with dreams. About five the last trace of sleep is exhausted, I just dream, which is more exhausting than wakefulness. In short, I spend the whole night in that state in which a healthy person finds himself for a short time before really falling asleep (*DI*, 74).

This last sentence alludes to an intermediate phase between wakefulness and sleep, which is the theater of hypnagogic images. In Kafka's case, instead of screening him from a state of complete wakefulness in order to lead him into a sound sleep, which is the normal function of these images, one may say their function was disrupted and that their very intensity repeatedly induced sudden returns to full consciousness, so that he vacillated ceaselessly between hypnagogic visions and wakeful dream fantasies.

What caused this exasperating attentiveness to dream images? Kafka reflected upon this question and concluded:

I believe this sleeplessness comes only because I write. For no matter how little and how badly I write, I am still made sensitive by these minor shocks, feel, especially toward evening and even more in the morning, the approaching, the imminent possibility of great moments which would tear me open, which could make me capable of anything, and in the general uproar that is within me and which I have no time to command, find no rest (*DI*, 74–75).

The next day Kafka was plagued by the same sleeplessness; the following gripping statement admirably sums up what he wrote in the citation immediately above:

Again it was the power of my dreams, shining forth into wakefulness even before I fall asleep, which did not let me sleep. In the evening and the morning my consciousness of the creative abilities in me is more than I can encompass. I feel shaken to the core of my being and can get out of myself whatever I desire (*DI*, 76).

The following month, he noted three more sleepless nights (*DI*, 152), and several days later: "As a result of the last few nights spent in wild dreams but with scarcely a few snatches of sleep, I was . . . incoherent this morning" (*DI*, 160).

The following year one finds the same kind of entries, for example: "I cannot sleep. Only dreams, no sleep" (*DI*, 291). Later he mentions this again briefly here and there (*DII*, 23, 39, 79) and it is not surprising that he also notes the occurrence of harassing headaches (*DII*, 114, 116, 118, 127, 140). Later on, in 1922, there is again a striking entry: "Almost impossible to sleep; plagued by dreams, as if they were being scratched on me, on a stubborn material" (*DII*, 218).

It is hardly astonishing, then, that in the same diaries, Kafka should note many times that he was exhausted and incapable of writing (*DI*, 39, 61, 152, 175, 202, 222, 227; *DII*, 31, 92, 95). One day at such a point he wrote: "I can't write any more. I've come up against the last boundary, before which I shall in all likelihood again sit down for years, and then in all likelihood begin another story all over again that will again remain unfinished" (*DII*, 98). (*There is still another curious parallel in the fact that many of Kafka's stories, notably* The Castle *and* Amerika, *like his engagements, failed to achieve full fruition.*) Several days after the incident mentioned above, however, inspiration returned (*DII*, 100). But the same anguish was destined to begin all over again. In December, 1914, the evening of the eighteenth, he wrote *The Giant Mole* "almost without knowing it, but was afraid to go on writing later than a quarter to two; the fear was well founded, I slept hardly at all, merely suffered through perhaps three short dreams and was then in the office in the condition one would expect" (*DII*, 103). Then again he found himself periodically incapable of writing (*DII*, 107, 111, 113, 119, 127, 128, 130).

Several times on the occasion of family difficulties, notably his father's illness in 1912, Franz was sharply urged to take charge of the family's business affairs during the free time that his work at the office permitted him in the afternoon.* Then, the scruples, the sense of guilt, the impulse towards self-defense doubled and tortured Franz to such a point that he was haunted by the vision of his own suicide. He saw himself leaping out of his window, and at the same time he categorically rejected the idea. He admitted this to Brod; the latter became frightened and warned Franz's mother. Without saying anything to his father, who was ill and not to be worried under any circumstances, she decided to arrange to have Franz replaced as manager of the factory. Equal claims were made on Franz by the family's business affairs during World War I.

As Franz approached the inevitable end of that torturous voyage, in spite of his continual alternation between hope and despair, creation and sterility, his situation grew still worse. On January 16, 1922, at the age of thirty-eight, he noted:

This past week I suffered something very like a breakdown; the only one to match it was on that night two years ago . . . Impossible to sleep, impossible to stay awake, impossible to endure life, or, more exactly, the course of life (*DII*, 201–02).

The reason for this, he said, was that the two "clocks" that regulated his life were not running in unison: the one regulating his external life where he pretended to live like everyone else "limps along at its usual speed," while the other regulating his inner life, "runs crazily on at a devilish or demoniac or in any case inhuman pace" (*DII*, 202). Among the reasons Kafka found to explain the demoniac pace, "the most obvious one," he said, "is introspection, which will suffer no idea to sink tranquilly to rest but must pursue each one into consciousness, only itself to become an idea, in turn to be pursued by renewed introspection" (*DI*, 202).

The term "idea" here embodies the term "image," for with Kafka the idea is always concrete. The idea departs from the image to which it imparts meaning. It is symbolic, that is to say

* According to Brod, the Insurance Institute office closed at two p. m. (*FK*, 79) [trans. note].

that it opens out upon something else while it suggests through a multiplicity of *correspondances** other images and ideas. Day and night, Kafka plunged recklessly into a jungle of such images. He explored its depths ceaselessly in the street and in his room, in visions that came to him from the outside as well as from his reveries, with such force, with such willful determination that at the moment when he should have fallen asleep he only increased his vigilance in order to capture the first hypnagogic images that came to him. When, exhausted, he tossed about in his sleep he seems to have been able to summon up a similar strength of will that enabled him consciously to seize while in a dream state those extraordinarily intense and precise dreams, accounts of which are scattered throughout the *Diaries*. If Kafka's short stories are incantatory and "hallucinatory" like dreams, it is because his dreams themselves were already short stories.

Halfway between the desk where Kafka did his writing and the bed where he dreamed more than he slept, special attention must be focused on that sofa where so often he stretched out at the end of the day to dream wide-awake. That sofa was an observatory where he lay in continual wait for the images that rise on the opposite horizons of waking and sleep. At times, with the sharpened insight of an invalid, he watches the interplay of light from the street as it transected lights and shadows inside the house (*DI*, 78). At other times he listens in a somnolent state to the voice of a young girl in the next room, constructing from the sound of her voice her actual appearance and then an imaginative vision of her (*DI*, 70). On still another occasion he loses

---

* An allusion to Baudelaire's poem "Correspondances" in *Les fleurs du mal*, in which the poet sets forth his concept of *correspondances*—a term derived from the vocabulary of the mystics—or the inextricable, harmonious interrelationship of all aspects of the Universe. This harmonious unity, perceptible to the human consciousness through an awareness of and a sensitivity to the interrelationship of the various sense impressions (synesthesia), may be given its fullest poetic expression through the adroit use of symbolic metaphor. This concept is fundamental to the French Symbolist movement and to much of twentieth-century literature in general [trans. note].

himself in a lengthy contemplation of clouds (*DII*, 200). On the opposite horizon the nocturnal images watch and wait. From the depths of the nocturnal world he receives a visit from a quasi-hallucinatory stranger seated in his room (*DII*, 201), or from the white horse that steps out of his head and jumps down from the bed (*DII*, 35). In midafternoon, as Kafka tries unsuccessfully to fall asleep, a wax woman lies on him and presses her left arm against his chest (*DI*, 152).

Stretched out, his eyes half-closed, Kafka slipped like a diver between two sheets of water towards the marvels and monsters of a twofold ocean of images, incurring the same risk of death that a deep-sea diver does.

Once more everything in Kafka's life coalesced in order to culminate in an inexorable process of self-destruction. In the center of it all, the most fearful power belongs to Kafka risen up against himself. How many people have considered Lautreamont's words on insomnia, Rimbaud's on hallucinations, Nerval's on the intrusion of the dream world into the world of wakefulness as some kind of literary game or as mere exaggeration? And would not the same be true of the importance the Surrealists attached to the revelation that comes in a state of "half-sleep"? One can say that Kafka died from having wished to sound the secret depths of these phenomena and to broaden their meaning beyond biologically permissible limits. At the risk of his life, he undertook to explore, alone and without a guide, a yoga of destruction. It was not he who had opened the abyss; it had been carved into his being from the outside. But he refused to flee from it or to cover it over, and he did his utmost to descend as deeply into it as he could before he drew his last breath.

The adventure of the mind into the depths of the consciousness is no less perilous than the adventure of the body into uncharted territory.

4

On the Side
of the Staff

As formidable as the power of solitude may have been for Kafka, it did not monopolize his life. The tragic tension in his destiny, on the contrary, derived from the opposition between his obstinate march into the mental wilderness on the one hand and his ardent participation in the social tragedy on the other.

He was very much interested in Gorky, Tolstoy, Herzen, Lenin, Kropotkin (*CWK*, 57–58; *DI*, 303). He frequented Czech political meetings, especially those of the anarchists (*FK*, 85–86; *CWK*, 53). Politics often turned up in his conversations with Janouch.

In order to understand exactly the range of Kafka's thought in the political domain, one must first grasp the thread of his social evolution. As one might expect, this also is to be found in the letter to his father. Kafka explains very clearly how he passed over the threshold of social awareness that would have ordinarily been closed to him by virtue of his social origins. His father's shop, which might have closed his eyes to such problems, was instead the locale of his first step toward a broader social awareness, because it had been first of all the locale of the initial break between him and his father. He wrote of the shop:

Things that had at first been a matter of course for me there, now began to torment and shame me, particularly the way you treated the staff . . . You I heard and saw shouting, cursing and raging in the shop, in a way that in my opinion at that time had not its equal anywhere in the world . . . You called the employees "paid enemies," and that was what they were too, but even before they became such you seemed to me to be their "paying enemy." There, too, I learned the great lesson that you could be unjust . . . Since however they were grown-up people, most of them with excellent nerves, they shook off this abuse without any trouble and in the end it did you much more harm than it did them. *But it made the business insuffer-able to me, reminding me far too much of my relations with you . . . That was why I could not but side with the staff . . .* [my italics] (*DF*, 161–62).

Hermann had not forseen this result, of course. Franz' discoveries in this realm were to increase and become more precise with age and professional experience. As an employee at the *Assicurazioni Generali*, he discovered a director as tyrannical as his father and quit the place (*DF*, 161). He then became a civil servant in the Workers' Accident Insurance Institute. The atmosphere there was quite different. Franz had scarcely begun work as a technical writer when he was called in to hear a pompous harangue by one of the directors. He burst into an uncontrollable frenzy of laughter. Happily the director concerned did not lack a sense of humor and the incident had no unpleasant consequences for Franz (*FK*, 87).

Despite Kafka's horror of the judicial mechanism that imprisoned him, despite his scruples with regard to the office, his superiors were very pleased with his work and remembered Kafka as being a man of exemplary devotion (*FK*, 82).

Kafka, then, can in no way be classed in the narrow category of introvert; he was as capable as anyone of taking part objectively in his work and of doing it efficiently. And his work also opened a new path of discovery and initiation. Employed in the accident prevention section of the Institute, he discovered in his work a hard social reality that amplified what he had noted in the relations between his father and the staff at the shop.

"A lot was expected of him [at the office]," writes Brod, "among other things jobs that he described—and this is the strongest word of disapproval I have ever heard from him—as 'disgusting,' as for example a kind of press campaign against not unjustified attacks to which social insurance was then exposed. This explains an entry in the diary, 'A sophistical article written for and against the institute' " (FK, 80).

Behind each dossier there was a living being—an accident victim or a widow. The true bureaucrat is unaware of this; he sees only forms to be filled out even when the victim sits before his desk. But no amount of forms and red tape, on the contrary, could keep Kafka from sensing the human drama of workers broken by machines and tortured by the hieroglyphs of legal language. Between the bureaucrat infatuated with his own sense of "facing realities" and Kafka the poet, which is the real introvert?

"His social conscience was greatly stirred when he saw workers crippled through neglect of safety precautions. 'How modest these men are,' he once said to me, opening his eyes wide. 'They come to us and beg. Instead of storming the institute and smashing it to little pieces, they come and beg' " (FK, 82).

Kafka knew how far the bitter blows of despair could drive a human being, and he could not resign himself to it:

Wept over the report of the trial of twenty-three-year-old Marie Abraham who, because of poverty and hunger, strangled her not quite nine-months-old child, Barbara, with a man's tie that she used as a garter (DI, 289).

Beneath Kafka's solitude rumbled the voice of the multitude. He is the mouthpiece of those who have no voice to make themselves heard.

In the network of meanings to be found in Kafka's work, the social meaning holds an important place. It is the most obvious, for beyond the other hidden meanings his work is first of all a portrait of the worker, alone, confronted with his job, unemployment, the city, mechanization, and bureaucracy, crushed between the necessity of earning his daily bread and the mysteries of an unfathomable and impersonal society.

The fact that neither rural life nor wild natural settings appear very often is significant in the work of a man who passionately loved excursions and travel. The setting of *The Trial* is composed almost uniquely of a labyrinth of sidestreets, courtyards, halls and rooms that communicate with one another. Even in *Amerika* when the hero is traveling on "The Road to Rameses" he is aware only of the gigantic immensity of metropolitan New York. *The Castle* should constitute an exception, since it takes place in a village, but in fact the action is confined within the streets and houses of the village, which, moreover, is buried under snow. In this respect, there exists in Kafka's work a curious thermal and mephitic symbolism of closed places inhabited by civil servants, as in the case of Klamm's heated sledge in *The Castle*, and the suffocating atmosphere that reigns in the courtroom, in the Law Court offices, or in the painter Titorelli's studio.*

In addition to the theme of the city, there is the theme of the mechanistic civilization represented by the role of the telephone in *The Trial*, *Amerika*, and especially *The Castle*, and by the marvelous desk of Karl's uncle and the puffing ascension of the large hotel's elevator in *Amerika*. In *The Penal Colony* the theme of torture by machine reaches the highest, most painful summit of both its mythical and its realistic implications. We have already discovered in it a constellation of sexual, legal, and sacred implications, but the existence of symbolic meanings in a work can never justify our overlooking the surface level of reality that is the basic source of any work's various symbolic levels. The terrifying machine in *The Penal Colony* is, first of all, simply a machine. How could Kafka not have been influenced, consciously or otherwise, by his awareness of the tragic relationship that unites the worker to his machine, where the machine, no longer satisfied with merely imposing an infinite series of brutalizing gestures, bites into the living flesh to mutilate or destroy it?

* *The Trial*, trans. Willa & Edwin Muir (New York: Knopf, 1960), pp. 47, 56, 78, 177.

In depicting the horror of the mechanistic age, Kafka equals or even surpasses Huxley in *Brave New World* and Butler in *Erewhon*. Once again Kafka sounds a warning for all of us, but this does not mean that he took a reactionary position, systematically denigrating the world of technology. On the contrary, Brod tells us that Kafka followed the development of technical progress with "inexhaustible curiosity," that he was passionately interested in the technological revolution, particularly in the newly developed fields of the cinema and aviation. Both men set out "with great enthusiasm" for the flying meet at Brescia in 1909 (*FK*, 102–103), after which Kafka wrote one of his first articles—delightfully humorous—on that festival in which Blériot, Curtiss, and other pioneers of nascent aviation took part.*

But none of these themes, the city, the office, the machine, suffices to exhaust the social reality of the modern world, which consists not only in a spectacle of objects, but also above all, in tragic conflicts in human relationships. Striking comparisons have been made between Kafka's nightmares and certain of the historical aberrations of our time, especially between *The Trial* and the Moscow trials of Stalin's day and between *The Penal Colony* and the Nazi concentration camps. Space certainly need not be wasted here in refuting the stupid calumnies according to which Kafka, by foreshadowing them, in some sense promoted these insane atrocities. Quite to the contrary, it was Kafka who sounded the alarm against them.

It may be more usefully pointed out that this prophetic aspect of Kafka's work did not derive from any magical powers of divination and does not apply solely to a few exceptionally monstrous incidents in recent history. The scope of Kafka's vision is rational and universal, born out of the pitiless analysis of oppressive phantasmagorias inherent in every bureaucratic power whether it be in private hands or state-controlled.

* This article, "The Aeroplanes at Brescia," is reprinted in an appendix to *The Penal Colony*, trans. Willa & Edwin Muir (New York: Schocken, 1961), pp. 297–309 [trans. note].

Critics have been correct in seeing in Kafka's evocation of the fearful power of the law an allusion to Mosaic law, both because of Kafka's Jewish background and because of the religious implications in his work, which will be discussed later on. But on the real and irreducible first plane of meaning he deals with the law in the ordinary sense of the word, and especially with "working class law," that is, those statutes that express and govern the interrelationship of powers between society in general and the mass of the workers. Insofar as this body of laws expresses a certain degree of protection against individual arbitrariness and "social scourges," they have a positive value. But insofar as laws tend to maintain fundamental injustices they also incorporate a repressive power within them. Even when these laws are protective, if they are couched in hermetic language, if they are irrelevant to concrete reality, if they are incomprehensible in their terminology and in the judicial decisions they inspire, then they retain their repressive power. Kafka often had occasion to verify this in the course of his experience at the Workers' Accident Insurance Institute.

True, this is only one limited area of possible indictment of the modern world, but it is symptomatic of flaws in the whole social structure. Everywhere in the modern world, between the bureaucrat and the governed, between the judge and the defendant, between the law and reality, between capital and labor, the truth of human relationships is enveloped in a formidable network of mysteries and mystifications. The vaporous cloud that invades the courtroom in *The Trial* gives us a striking image of these "mysteries" that blur the obvious in an epoch that thought it had banished all mystery.

Kafka's work, in reflecting this situation derives a double aspect from it. On the one hand the social situation holds an immense and entirely real place. One actually finds a worker seeking to be hired, a defendant attempting to defend himself, an immigrant in search of his place in a new world. If these stories have a fantastic atmosphere, it is because they are faithful to reality. The social reality of the here and now is inherently as phantasmagoric as the reality of any ancient or exotic world. But for our lethargic social consciences we would see this fact for ourselves, but one of the primary functions of Kafka's "nightmares" is to shake us out of our torpor and awaken us to such an awareness.

On the other hand it is because the immediate and "banal" world is filled with emanations of the fantastic that Kafka is able symbolically to evoke other mysteries for us, mysteries that date from time immemorial, and although their manifestations are necessarily refracted in our present-day society, they will survive that society because their origins lie in the unfathomable depths of destiny. For this reason, Kafka has been able to give us in modern form the contemporary equivalent of what the tales from folklore, the Homeric epics, *The Thousand and One Nights*, the Arthurian romances, or *Don Quijote* were for their times.

It is not by chance that so many great themes from ancient epics are to be found in Kafka's tales: the inaccessible "castle" and the "metamorphosis" in the stories of these titles, the messenger and the gigantic edifices (*The Wall of China*), the impossible thirst for justice (*The Trial*), the rites of initiation (*A Hunger Artist*), the paternal curse (*The Judgment*), the voyage to a new world (*Amerika*), the descent into hell ("I Was a Visitor Among the Dead"), the ritual sacrifice (*The Penal Colony*), etc.

All of these themes are at the same time archaic, modern, and futuristic, for they are so many indestructible configurations of men's destinies. But the use Kafka made of them is very personal. He had nothing in common with latter-day Classicists who plagiarize outdated literary forms; in parting from present-day reality he is directly re-creating mythical themes. Thereby he raises that reality to the same sublime rank as ancient images of destiny, and thus he unveils the universal, symbolic scope of reality.

All too few writers have understood that social struggles were the great literary subject of our era and that the proletarian hero was as worthy of new epics as the heroes of other times. Kafka did understand this and, if he does not paint great collective frescoes as Zola did in *Germinal,* he evokes the individual's adventure as Homer did in the Odyssey. By the elimination of all insignificant details, by the absolute, poetic *necessity* of his style, by deploying a majestic choreography of destiny, Kafka succeeded in imparting to his heroes the exemplary significance of epic heroes.

But he effects a complete transfer of the grandeur that formerly emanated from the higher social planes, down into the world of the laborer. His hero is neither a demigod nor a king nor a knight nor even the hero of the bourgeois novel. The hero of *The Castle* is not the castellan–landowner but the unemployed surveyor; the hero of *The Trial* is not the judge but the fallen chief clerk of the bank; or he is a traveling salesman *(The Metamorphosis),* a bell-hop *(Amerika),* a tenant, an employee.

With this perspective it is entirely reasonable that one may not even glimpse the faces of the great of this world in Kafka's stories. The judges of the High Court, the gentleman of the Castle, are not men that one may see or approach; they are as inaccessible as the Emperor of China. One can barely imagine their existence on the other side of a sea of clouds that swathe and conceal them from alien eyes. That also is a social reality, for employees know only by hearsay the occult entities who serve on boards of directors.

Thus one should not be surprised that the "Castle" does not resemble a castle, but "a rambling pile consisting of innumerable small buildings," or for that matter that the "courthouse" is not an imposing monument but resembles a great warehouse on the city's fringe, whose entrance looks like a truck loading-door and in which other doors are inscribed with the names of commercial firms of which Joseph K. knows through his bank. For Kafka is depicting the fortresses of the industrial world. In opposition to the Gothic novel, the secret of the "Castle" is not at all some old feudal mystery, the secret of some mighty lord, but the mystery and secretiveness of the corporation and of the government bureaucracy where the worker, whether he be employee or supplicant citizen, never meets anyone with whom he can speak man to man. Everything there is directed by anonymous and collective orders from above that move the world like the blind powers of Fatality.

Even these orders are diffused behind the all too familiar hierarchy of civil servants who occupy the middle rungs of the ladder, where they are supposed to link the higher echelons with the lower ones, but where they more than likely obstruct communication between them. This intermediate class of civil servants is precisely the one to which Kafka belonged by virtue of his profession; yet it was a permanent target of his attacks.

Kafka describes neither strikes nor collective struggles nor any great surge of the masses nor even tragic individual adventures such as the story of Marie Abraham. Karl Rossmann is simply a young man who migrates from one menial job to another; K., a surveyor looking for work. Even Joseph K. enters into the center of the bloody tragedy only at the last moment, having previously lived an interminable series of peripatetic adventures whose gravity is not evident at first sight.

Kafka's great subject is ordinary life itself, but his revelation consists of showing that nothing is more extraordinary than this supposedly ordinary life, for it is the arena where a prodigious social fantasy is played out. If we become fully aware of its existence only with difficulty it is because we ourselves are enmeshed in the process like the figures in an immense tapestry. The role of the revolutionary, and of Kafka, is to permit us for an instant, through our imagination, to place ourselves at a distance in order that we may begin to see the weave and design of the tapestry and our place in it.

Marx emphasized and reemphasized in his works, even in *Das Kapital*, the extreme importance of the phantasmagoric in social relationships. It is one of the fundamental bases of his dialectic. However, since he was primarily an economist and a political thinker Marx did not develop this particular aspect of his thought as he did the others. Such an undertaking is the domain of psychologists and artists. It is on precisely this aspect of

social relationships that Kafka sheds the strongest light. As a result, individualistic and personal as his work is, it is at the same
time a virulent criticism of society.

This fact is all the more remarkable since by virtue of his
bourgeois family background, his law studies, his position as a
civil servant, Kafka was on the side of the "gentlemen"; he was
one of the initiates into the mysteries of the law and of capital.
But he transformed his personal trials into a number of socially
revealing experiences that were for him literally rites of initiation, since they enabled him to cross the psychological barriers
blocking the view of the social fantasy and permitted him to
pass over the threshold of social taboos that masked from him
the reality of the human world.

But Georges Bataille, the left-wing critic, objects. In an often
excellent article in which he comments on my previous study
of Kafka, he maintains that Kafka's attitude was merely an expression of childishness and submissiveness, and that he rejected
reason and effective action in such a way that from a revolutionary point of view he can only be "condemned."*

The Communist Party, Bataille writes, "is a party that respects
reason alone, that sees only concealed private interest in irrational values that foster a luxurious, useless, childish way of life.
The only single overriding attitude admissible in the Communist
framework is the child's, but in his *minor* state where such an
attitude is conceded to children who cannot rise to an adult level
of seriousness. The adult who ascribes inordinate significance to
childishness, who approaches literature with the feeling of
touching upon the supreme value, has no place in the Communist
society. In a world where bourgeois individualism is banished,
the inexplicable, puerile ill-humor of the adult Kafka is inde-
fensible. Communism is in its very principle negation realized,
the contrary of the meaning of Kafka's words" (*Ibid.*, 182).

This point of view seems to me untenable. Let us not deceive

* Georges Bataille, *La Littérature et le mal* (Paris: Gallimard, 1957),
pp. 161–82.

ourselves, moreover, when Bataille assures us that Kafka is to be condemned, that he is pervaded with puerility, laziness, and uselessness, this does not mean that Bataille is against Kafka. On the contrary, Bataille is always on the side of puerility, laziness, and uselessness, and he adores being guilty. We think he exaggerates sometimes—here in any case.

As for art as the supreme value for the artist, Marx did not at all profess a sectarian, propagandistic point of view, as the following admirable passage bears witness: "The writer in no way regards his works as a *means*. They are *ends in themselves;* so little are they a means for him and others that, when necessary, he sacrifices *his* existence to *theirs*, and, like the preacher of religion, he takes as his principle: 'Obey God more than men . . . ,' "* a statement that applies perfectly to Kafka who, to put it precisely, sacrificed his life to his work.

Yet it is true that there exists an extraordinary "childhood spirit" in Kafka, and that this state of mind goes completely beyond ordinary limits—the letter to his father shows this clearly —but the very way in which he takes cognizance of it is entirely contrary to any kind of childishness, and the way in which he broke out of his family's sphere of thought to practice his profession and to become aware of the "other side" of social problems represents a categorical rejection of puerility.

Finally, can it be said that Kafka expresses nothing but an attitude of submissiveness? Even with regard to his father this is not so. He was affectionate, his spirit was half-broken, but there was an unbreakable, pitiless, sometimes even deliberately provoking side to him. Moreover, one cannot draw a point for point parallel between his attitude toward social problems and his attitude toward his family. Nor can one identify Kafka absolutely with his heroes: K., Joseph K., and the others need make no gesture of rebellion, the very oppression they suffer calls

* "The Writer's Profession," in Karl Marx and Frederick Engels, *Literature and Art: Selections from their Writings* (New York: International Publishers, 1947), p. 63.

forth a sense of revulsion, and the terrifying description of their oppressive worlds is a mark of the total significance of Kafka's thought.

His thought is both complex and subtle. One becomes easily convinced of this in rereading the conversations with Janouch when Kafka talks about Taylorism (*CWK*, 68, 69), or propaganda images (*Ibid.*, 86), or the League of Nations (*Ibid.*, 74, 75), or the Russian Revolution (*Ibid.*, 70, 71, 72). He nearly always emphasized the antinomic aspects of these questions, that is to say, the dialectic tension inherent in the continuous progression of human life.

Characteristically, in the Revolution of 1917 Kafka saw an attempt to construct "an absolutely just world," but he also saw the peril of a new war of religion unleashed on humanity (*CWK*, 70), an all the more depressing prospect since he perceived the antinomic aspect of the workers' emancipation: "Behind them already," he remarked to Janouch, "are the secretaries, officials, professional politicians, all the modern satraps for whom they are preparing the way to power . . . At the end of every truly revolutionary development there appears a Napoleon Bonaparte . . . The Revolution evaporates and leaves behind only the slime of a new bureaucracy. The chains of tormented mankind are made out of red tape" (*CWK*, 71).

In 1920, when Franz Kafka made that sinister statement, it would have been easy to accuse him of petty bourgeois scepticism. But since Khrushchev's official declaration of the crimes of Stalin, it is certain that the contradictions between the working class and its bureaucrats have not all been rendered harmonious, and that detailed clarification of such questions is the major problem for the future of working-class emancipation.

Kafka never turned his face away from the seriousness of the social drama. The apparent resignation of his heroes before the powers that overwhelm them only takes on its full ironic sense when one brings to bear the brief notations in which Kafka brutally expressed the bitterness of the social struggle, as in this sketch:

The director of the Progress Insurance Company was always greatly dissatisfied with his employees. Now every director is dissatisfied with his employees; the difference between employees and directors is too vast to be bridged by means of mere commands on the part of director and mere obedience on the part of the employees. Only mutual hatred can bridge the gap and give the whole enterprise its perfection (*DII*, 73).

The humor at the end detracts in no way from the story's acerbic sharpness. Another case in point is this sketch for *The Castle* in which the same director receives an applicant for the position of office attendant:

"You're tall enough," he said, "I can see that; but what can you do? Our attendants must be able to do more than lick stamps . . . Naturally, we can employ only people who are in good health. Before you are taken on you will have to be examined by the doctor. You are quite well now? Really? Of course, that could be. Speak up a little! Your whispering makes me nervous . . . And now go, go. Trembling like that won't do you any good. I have no authority to hand out favors. You're willing to do any kind of work? Certainly. Everyone is. That's no special distinction. It merely indicates the low opinion you have of yourself . . . (*DII*, 74).

This scene is taken from daily life, and yet it is completely fantastic. One could easily clear up all the mystifications surrounding Kafka's work if one could see that *The Castle* is written with the same ink as this sketch and is no more fantastic than reality itself and that it overflows with an indignation that is all the more violent for being suppressed. Does one take Jarry for an admirer of Ubu?* It is up to the reader to decide and to draw the consequences.**

Who can fail to understand this upon hearing, in the sketch

* Ubu, the farcio-satirical main character in Alfred Jarry's play *Ubu Roi*, is an ambiguous figure who seems to embody all the faults of the stolid bourgeois and yet possesses a frightening lucidity with regard to the absurdity of the human condition [trans. note].

** Moreover, a parallel can be drawn between Chaplin's clown, Jaroslav Hasek's "brave soldier Schweik," and Kafka's K. We cannot develop this comparison here, but it suffices to say that there is no reason whatsoever for indicting Kafka in particular on this score.

"New Lamps" (in *DF*, 111–13), the director's speech in reply to the claims of a delegation of miners? Here is the end of it:

But here is something for you to tell your workmates downstairs: We here shall not rest until we have made a drawing-room of your shaft, and if you do not all finally go to your doom in patent-leather shoes, then you shall not go at all.

The real paradox of Kafka is that, although he was capable of writing words of terrible cruelty, he preached no hatred. So far as he was concerned, nothing could be decisively set right until everything were ordered according to the dictates of justice, and not only must the ends be just but the means to those ends as well. Up to now, at least, we know only a few of his all too brief allusions to the dialectic between force and destiny, between liberty and submission. These allusions, which Janouch recorded, can best be understood by comparing them to Ghandi's principles. How many times did one hear Ghandi belittled as the prototype of the ineffectual idealist? It was Ghandi, however, who liberated India. So in Kafka's submissiveness there was as much resistance to submission as there was violence in Ghandi's nonviolence.

Kafka's work is indeed the most intimate and most unusual of confidences. It is also a social satire of a kind without precedent, the first stark revelation of the social phantasmagoria. We are far from having exhausted its content.

5

The Land of Canaan

We have observed the rise of the double edifice, as closely joined as Siamese twins yet mutually inimical, of Kafka's interior and exterior worlds. Their foundations are laid deep within the earth, but their outlines are silhouetted against the heaven of the Absolute.

Determinedly terrestial, Kafka's seemingly fantastic works pose the enigma of the human condition in all its breadth. On this major point there can be no doubt. But does not Kafka's work seem as enigmatic as the enigma it poses? Has it not given rise to infinitely contradictory commentaries on the part of his critics? All too often these contradictions reflect an error in method. Before "judging" Kafka's thought, before confronting his thought with that of other writers, one must first interpret Kafka in the light of Kafka himself, that is to say, in terms of the general direction of his spiritual evolution.

The indisputable fact that Kafka, born a Jew, grew up in the Jewish faith must be taken as the initial point of departure. Did he hold on to that conception of the world and of the Absolute, or did he reject it? In seeking the answer to this question, the letter to his father is once more a document of inestimable value:

As a child I reproached myself, in accord with you, for not going to the synagogue enough, for not fasting, and so on. I thought that in this way I was doing a wrong not to myself but to you, and I was penetrated by a sense of guilt, which was, of course, always ready to hand (*DF*, 171–172).

He received nothing then in the way of a truly religious up-bringing, but instead a dull mixture composed of a sense of ritual and a sense of guilt associated with failure to observe the rituals—a situation, moreover, in which he did not differ from a great number of young Christians:

Later, as a boy, I could not understand how, with the insignificant scrap of Judaism you yourself possessed, you could reproach me for not . . . making an effort to cling to a similar insignificant scrap. It was indeed really, so far as I could see, a mere scrap, a joke, not even a joke (*DF*, 172).

There follows a cruel description of the Jewish ceremonies, in which Franz is seen in the synagogue bored to death and merely daydreaming. At home, family religious rites degener-ated into a comedy accompanied by wild laughter. Again there are obvious parallels with what takes place in a number of sup-posedly Christian homes.

And so there was the religious material that was handed to me . . . How one could do anything better with this material than get rid of it as fast as possible was something I could not understand; precisely getting rid of it seemed to me the most effective act of "piety" one could perform (*DF*, 173).

Kafka realized, however, that in spite of that degradation his father's Judaism was not entirely "a mere scrap":

You had really brought some traces of Judaism with you from that ghetto-like little village community . . . (*DF*, 173).

But what Hermann had received was too moribund to be transmitted to Franz: ". . . It was too little to be handed on to the child; it all dribbled away while you were passing it on" (*DF*, 174). At this point it seemed then that Kafka was to follow the usual road of all those who break away from their childhood beliefs—or rather the shadows of beliefs—to become firmly en-trenched in agnosticism or even in atheism.

In fact, the process had already begun in early childhood, since the son had become totally aware of having received only scraps of Judaism without substance and without faith. But suddenly, in the midst of that long slippage, which carried him always further from Judaism, a change took place. Kafka underwent a rebirth of interest in "Jewish things." This expression may seem rather insipid and to concern no more than an intellectual curiosity, but Kafka's interest went much further: *"It was, after all, Judaism of your Judaism that was here stirring . . . my new Judaism"* [my italics] (*DF*, 175–76).

This remark is of incalculable importance. In retrospect it reveals to us that what Kafka had once taken for dead within himself was not so dead. What he had taken for the annihilation of faith was only a wintertime of faith, for the supposedly dead tree, good only to be thrown into the fire, was now beginning to put forth new leaves. It is true that this reawakening was not due to his father's influence, but rather to the establishment of new Jewish friendships. But for them, it is likely that the tree, deprived of nourishment, would eventually have withered and died. Yet how could these friendships have had such an influence on Kafka if he had not himself been born into Judaism?

The crowning irony is that Franz' new interest in Jewish things, instead of bringing him closer to his father, had quite the opposite effect. The father was irritated by the "new Judaism" that he saw growing in his son and in which he had no direct part. This unhappy state of affairs was sufficient to cause Kafka to write: "Through my mediation Judaism became abhorrent to you and Jewish writings [became] unreadable; they 'nauseated' you" (*DF*, 176). This is proof enough that Franz was right when he maintained that his father was familiar with little more than "scraps" of Judaism.

Thus there was no way of bringing about a reconciliation with his father. In the first instance, the struggle against an empty faith was a struggle against his father; in the second, the struggle for faith became also a struggle against his father.

In any case, Kafka was literally on the road to conversion.
He turned toward Judaism as others have turned toward Christianity. This does not mean that he was a sort of Jewish equivalent to Huysmans, Léon Bloy, or Germain Nouveau.* Kafka
does not speak of any radical conversion, but of a renewal of
Judaism that stirred within him, *striving to be born.*

This is enough to show that Kafka cannot be considered an
atheist, but it is not enough to make a true believer of him. Even
less did he seek the easy comfort of skepticism. Thrown into
the heart of the spiritual combat, Kafka remained poised between faith and negation of faith. Kafka's duel with the Absolute is all the more difficult to grasp since it takes place on a
vaster plane than that of a simple confrontation between Judaism and its negation. Christian thought also intervenes in the
conflict.

Kafka was deeply interested not only in Kierkegaard but also
in Dostoevski. He read Pascal closely (*DII*, 173) and Léon Bloy
(*KMD*, 48). He was not in principle hostile to Christianity or
even to Roman Catholicism; from time to time he made incisive
allusions to them, which are those of an outsider who has many
times circled about their perimeters (*DI*, 301; *DII*, 17; *CWK*,
62–63, 92, 93).

The most remarkable of these brief notations is doubtless the
following:

We too must suffer all the suffering around us. Christ suffered for
mankind, but mankind must suffer for Christ (*DF*, 46, 97).

This statement is so profoundly Christian that it might well
be appended to the writings of the saints, who wished to suffer
in order to join in the suffering of Christ and in that of all men,
as Christ had wished to share in all human suffering. While this
is the only time that Kafka went so far in this direction, one
can neither deny the statement nor generalize upon it. In his

* J. K. Huysmans (1848–1907), Léon Bloy (1846–1917), and Germain
Nouveau (1852–1920): French writers who underwent radical conversion
to Roman Catholicism [trans. note].

works one does find other traces of a "temptation" toward Christianity. It cannot be entirely by chance that there is a chapel (an unusual fact in itself) in the uncle's house in *Amerika*,* and that the cathedral plays a strangely important role in *The Trial* where an unusual association of symbols is developed. Through the appearance of the themes of the Italian, of night, of the Knight's armor, of the lone priest in the deserted cathedral, *The Trial* plunges us into an atmosphere very like that of the Gothic novel, which, it seems to me, is generally marked by a nostalgic hostility toward Roman Catholicism. Here Kafka wanders mentally with Joseph K. in the sacred world of Catholicism, but only at night, with a peculiar mixture of defensiveness and exotic seduction. (In this instance, Kafka's mythical identification with his hero was conscious enough that he could write, one day in 1922: "Despite my having legibly written down my name, despite their having correctly written to me twice already, they have Joseph K. down in the directory. Shall I enlighten them or shall I let them enlighten me?" (*DII*, 213).

Kafka's spiritual horizon extends, moreover, very far in all directions. In his work one finds many allusions to diverse esoteric doctrines, notably to the old Indian and Platonic theory of the transmigration of souls. He confessed to Janouch one day that he felt both repelled and attracted by India:

All these Yogis and sorcerers rule over the life of nature not because of their burning love of freedom but because of a concealed and icy hatred of life. The source of Indian religious devotions is a bottomless pessimism (*CWK*, 53).

This judgment, while perhaps excessively harsh, is nonetheless typical of Kafka's personal attitude. Notwithstanding admitted appearances, he violently rejected every systematically pessimistic conception of life.

The same mixture of attraction and revulsion typifies Kafka's

* The chapel is not in Uncle Jacob's house but in Mr. Pollunder's suburban mansion; see *Amerika* (Garden City, N. Y.: Doubleday, 1946), p. 74 [trans. note].

reaction to the theosophy, or more particularly the "anthro-posophy," of Dr. Rudolf Steiner, whom he met one day in Berlin (*DI*, 54ff.). He expressed his fear that Steiner's doctrine would only result in new confusion for him.

On the other hand, Kafka's interest in the esoteric aspects of Judaism, especially the Kabbala and Hasidism, seem much closer to the mainstream of his life. After several isolated allusions (*DI*, 166; *DII*, 119), he goes so far as to declare that if Zionism had not intervened, all his writing might have led to a new secret doctrine, a "Kabbalah" (*DII*, 203).

This last declaration, made in 1922, strongly reinforces what he said in 1919, in the letter to his father, concerning his "new Judaism." The relationship with Judaism is, then, the funda-mental problem that one must examine in order to understand Kafka's spiritual itinerary.

In speaking of the origin of this revival of interest, the letter to his father alludes only to certain friendships, but Brod reveals that they were numerous and active. Whatever may be truly and tragically said about the existence of Kafka's profound inner solitude, it must never cause one to lose sight of the fact that, for all his solitude, he was no less a very sociable and lively person. It would be entirely erroneous to think of him as always tense, taciturn, morose, and lost in the lugubrious meditation of a misanthrope: ". . . It was a great happiness to live in Kafka's neighborhood and to enjoy at first hand his lively thoughts as they bubbled forth—even his hypochondria was still entertain-ing and full of ideas" (*FK*, 115).

Kafka loved to take advantage of his vacations in order to travel, often with Brod, in Austria, Switzerland, Germany, Italy, and France. In the course of his daily existence in Prague he frequented many cafés and went to lectures and the theater. He made a number of friends. Besides Brod, the novelist, there were Félix Weltsch, the philosopher, and Oscar Baum, the poet, who were his most intimate acquaintances. Others whom Kafka fre-quented were the writers Martin Buber, Franz Werfel, Otto

Pick, Ernest Weiss, Willy Haas, and Rudolf Fuchs,* and the actors M. and Mme. Klug, M. and Mme. Tchissik, and above all, Isak Löwy (FK, 108–11). Apart from Franz Werfel, who became well known after World War II for his Song of Bernadette, and Martin Buber, these names will probably have little meaning for most readers; Kafka's meeting such people, however, is extremely significant in his destiny, for they were part of the elite of the central European Jewish intelligentsia.

Kafka met Löwy and the actors of his troupe in 1910, and he mentions them often in the diary of 1911, where one is immediately struck by his interest in the theater. Many of the scenes in his stories, especially A Fratricide, are in fact described as though seen by a spectator in a theater. But Kafka had a special interest in Löwy's troupe, for they performed only popular Jewish plays in Yiddish. Kafka was deeply interested in the folkloric, linguistic, and religious aspects of the troupe's repertory and what it expressed concerning the Jewish spirit in the diaspora. Furthermore, this troupe had come from eastern Europe, and as Kafka came to know Löwy more intimately the latter made known to him a wealth of details surrounding the customs and the spiritual crisis of the Jewish world in Poland and Russia (FK, 112ff.), Kafka thus gained a deeper knowledge of Hasidism, the great Jewish mystical movement of eastern Europe, first of all through Löwy in 1911 (DI, 166), then through popular meetings organized among Eastern and Western Jews in 1915 (DII, 117, 119). In that same year Kafka met Langer, a Kabbalistic writer and practicing Hasidist, who introduced him to a Hasidic rabbi and explained a number of points concerning the history and the mystique of the movement (DII, 128, 138–39). Kafka also knew Martin Buber, the most world-renowned of the Hasidic writers. In 1922, Kafka plunged into one of Buber's works on Hasidism (DII, 229).

* Rudolf Fuchs' "Reminiscences of Franz Kafka" have been published as an appendix to the second edition of Brod's biography Franz Kafka (New York, 1960), pp. 255–58 [trans. note].

By definition, Hasidism is a movement of mystical devotion. Jewish history has known several manifestations of it. The contemporary (and the most important) one, which flourished in eastern Europe in Kafka's day, was founded in the eighteenth century by Israel Baal Shem.* Serouya tends to insist upon the "illuminated" and at the same time "obscurantist" side of Hasidic practices (p. 456), but the best aspect of the movement is strongly emphasized by Scholem, who characterizes it in a very interesting way by stressing the similarities and differences between Hasidism and the Kabbala:

"In the Hasidic movement," Scholem writes, "Kabbalism appears no longer in a theosophic guise, or to be more exact, theosophy with all its complicated theories, if it is not entirely dropped, is at least no longer the focal point of the religious consciousness . . . Hasidism is practical mysticism at its highest . . . To put it as briefly as possible, the distinctive feature of the new school is to be found in the fact that the secrets of the divine realm are presented in the guise of mystical psychology. It is by descending into the depths of his own self that man wanders through all the dimensions of the world; in his own self he lifts the barriers which separate one sphere from the other; in his own self, finally, he transcends the limits of natural existence and at the end of his way, without, as it were, a single step beyond himself, he discovers that God is 'all in all' and there is 'nothing but Him' " (pp. 340–41).

These successive stages and transformations are accompanied by a veritable "emotional enthusiasm":

"When he fulfills the commandments or studies the Torah, the body becomes a throne of the soul . . . and the soul a throne for the light of the Shekhinah** which is above his head, and the

---

* Henri Serouya, *La Kabbale: ses origines, sa psychologie, sa mystique, sa métaphysique* (Paris: Grassett, 1941), p. 444; and Gershom Gerhard Scholem, *Major Trends in Jewish Mysticism,* (New York: Schocken, 1954), p. 325.

** The Divine Manifestation, through which God's presence is felt by man.

light as it were flows all round him, and he sits in the midst
of the light and rejoices in trembling' " (pp. 335–36).

Whatever the degree of influence of Hasidism on Kafka, it is
certain that he gave it lengthy and keen attention. It is equally
certain that there exist curious parallels between Hasidism and
Kafka's extreme interest in states of illumination and the inner
pilgrimage of the self up to the threshold of the indestructible.*
But let us not anticipate, for, in the meantime, we must recall
other Judaic currents that intervene as deeply in Kafka's work.

During these same years, in fact, the Zionist movement was
also in full sway. Several thousands of Jews had already emi-
grated to Palestine, then a colony of the Turkish Empire, and
the international organization of the movement was progressing
bit by bit. In 1913, the question of Zionism was ardently
discussed in Kafka's intellectual milieu. There were long discussions between Buber, Werfel, Brod, Pick, Baum, and Kafka.
Brod was for the movement; Kafka was undecided. "Conversation about feelings of community," Brod noted at the time,
"Kafka says he has none, because his strength just about suffices
for himself alone" (FK, 113). These discussions became so lively
at times that they provoked a certain misunderstanding. But
Kafka evolved and became favorably disposed toward Zionism.
The collapse of the Turkish Empire at the end of World War I
and the famous Balfour Declaration of 1917 made possible the
founding of the Jewish National Committee in Palestine, and
Zionism thus gained new impetus. Brod played a militantly
active role in the movement during the years 1918 and 1919, and
Kafka stood by him "with advice, interest, encouragement, and
loving agreement . . ." (FK, 113).

Kafka's extraordinary outline of a project for a "Brotherhood
of Poor Workers" seems also to have been formulated around
1918 (DF, 103–105). This community would be essentially

---

* Kafka's own term, to which he refers in the aphorisms contained in
"Reflections on the Way and the Life, etc." (DF, 39, 42 passim.). See also,
the present work, pp. 108, 110–11ff [trans. note].

founded on a spirit of poverty, its members assuring their sub-
sistance only through labor (intellectual or manual) and for "no
wages other than what is necessary to support life . . . for two
days." For their personal use, they would have only the absolute
necessities, eating nothing but bread, water, and dates, "Food as
eaten by the poorest of the poor," and living in the humblest of
shelters. They would locate "In places where one can help, in
abandoned districts, almshouses, [as a] teacher." The rule of the
community would be founded on honesty and conscientious-
ness with no intervention of the courts being invoked.

This plan may be explained in part by Kafka's taste for a
vegetarian diet as well as by his social ideals. But this explanation
alone is not sufficient; Kafka's brotherhood is clearly an admirable transposition of the "vow of poverty" taken by monks—all
the more admirable considering the many flagrant violations of
this vow by monastic orders during their periodic times of material prosperity.

The "rule" devised by Kafka, on the contrary, assures in
detail that the state of poverty in his brotherhood shall be as
rigorous as that of a newly formed monastic order. Even more
striking is the similarity between Kafka's clear-sightedness and
that of Father de Foucauld, who before his death in 1916 had
abandoned the real but archaic poverty of the Trappists in order
to share the present-day poverty of the proletariat, and had
eventually left France to live in the most remote region of the
Sahara.*

The simultaneity of these two outcries of alarm and love are
the more moving for having passed completely unnoticed at the
time. This coincidence is less odd than it seems at first sight,
however, because in both cases their attitudes stem from the
same primary source: the appeal of the prophets of Israel for
their people to accept poverty. In Kafka's case it seems impossible, besides, not to think that there may have been a link between this project and the idea of the Kibbutzim, the Zionist

* See Michel Carrouges, *Foucauld devant l'Afrique du Nord* (Paris:
Editions du Cerf, 1961).

labor cooperatives that were centers of spiritual and material reconquest of the Promised Land.*

Though never realized, Kafka's project holds a significant place in his thought. But his return to Judaism was not restricted merely to contacts with Jewish friends, nostalgic longings and impulsive projects. It was manifested also in a very concrete way, first of all in a consuming interest in the Hebrew language: in 1918, at thirty-five years of age, Kafka took Hebrew lessons (*FK*, 168). He worked at it with such dogged devotion during his last years that, after his death, "of the papers he left behind, the papers filled with Hebrew exercises are not much fewer than those covered with literary works in German" (*FK*, 197).

Moreover, during a trip to Germany he formed a keen fondness for the Berlin Jewish People's Home, organized by a Dr. Lehmann, on which both he and Brod founded great hopes. He even urged Felicia, his fiancée, to enroll as a volunteer worker at the Home (*FK*, 196).

His renascent Judaism grew in all directions. The Land of Canaan burned afar with the light of a thousand fires and shone upon him. Where would this many-sided spiritual quest lead him?

* Compare Kafka's reflections on Father Flanagan's Boys' Town in Omaha, Nebraska (*CWK*, 70).

The Trap of
Eternal Postponement

Where can one find a darker picture of life than in Kafka's tales? In no other fictional world does man seem to be more totally crushed by fate. Is his not indeed a universe of despair?

Even in *Amerika*, the most "juvenile," the most agile of his novels, the hero is unjustly persecuted. The story was to have been completed, it seems, but one of life's supreme cruelties did not permit the author to achieve this task; it was beyond his strength. Everywhere life leads to an ultimate condemnation. In *The Castle*, the Land Surveyor, K., does not succeed either in getting orders to go to work or in obtaining permission to enter the castle. Again, the novel is unfinished and leaves no room for hope. According to Brod's indications, Kafka planned for the Land Surveyor in the end at least to obtain permission to live and work in the village; but would this not have been a supreme mockery, since the permission would not have been granted him until he was already dying of exhaustion? Joseph K., the hero of *The Trial*, accused of he knows not what, is prosecuted by a caricature of justice and brutally executed. *The Penal Colony* is nothing less than a horrible evocation of a torture machine on which the judge himself commits suicide. *The Judgment* and *A Country Doctor* also end with what amount to death sentences. Through a monstrous illness that reduces

Gregor Samsa to the state of a vermin, *The Metamorphosis* evokes the most degrading torture prolonged to the very death. It is the link that binds together the three short stories *Investigations of a Dog, The Burrow,* and *Josephine the Singer, or the Mouse Folk* in which the nobility of the human condition is pared down to a level of powerlessness, that of a dog, a badger, and a mouse.

There is no recourse, no hope. It would be too little to say that hope is vain; it is dried up at the source. And yet one recalls Kafka's uncontrollable laughter in the middle of a solemn discourse by one of his superiors (*FK*, 87). The remarkable thing is that he bursts into the same kind of laughter in face of the dark solemnity of his own fictional universe. Brod writes:

"It is a new kind of smile that distinguishes Kafka's work, a smile close to the ultimate—a metaphysical smile so to speak— indeed sometimes when he used to read out one of his tales for us friends of his, it rose above a smile and we laughed aloud" (*FK*, 133).

"Thus, for example, we friends of his laughed quite immoderately when he first let us hear the first chapter of *The Trial.* And he himself laughed so much that there were moments when he couldn't read any further" (*FK*, 178).

Breton was not wrong then to include Kafka in his gallery of masters of black humor.* One has only to look at photographs of Kafka, moreover, in order to see that there was no lugubrious or defeatist air about him. And so, in the immense nightmare of his tales, streaks of wild laughter burst forth. Each time the dark spell is broken; we have invasions of beds in the schoolroom (*The Castle*) and in the chambers of the "courthouse" (*The Trial*), the clownish rôle of the Land Surveyor's assistants and the pompous harangue of the Mayor (*The Castle*). The executioner and the police are hidden in a storage room of

---

*André Breton, *Anthologie de l'humour noir* (Paris: Jean-Jacques Pauvert, [1966]), pp. 439–60 [André Breton (1896–1966) was the leader of the French surrealist movement and author of, among other works, the surrealist novel *Nadja* (trans. note).]

the bank like a jack-in-the-box or like Punchinello in a cupboard. Kafka's work is truly a nightmare, but one shot through with the barbs of parody.

Even when he depicts the most overwhelming horror, the artist himself refuses to be entirely overcome by it. He dominates it in that he unmasks it and presents it as a re-creation of his own mind.

The moment Kafka evokes his own life of unspeakable suffering, he projects it beyond himself, cloaking objective reality in the form of a deliberate nightmare, a formidable caricature. This terrible spiritual travail is by definition a deliverance from pain. Rising above the entire scene in order to contemplate it, the artist dominates his own creation.

It must follow, then, that his work teaches us a similar lesson: before our eyes Kafka lifts the veil of unconsciousness that hid from us the social pantomine and the human condition itself; he violently reveals to us the pitiless tragedy that we did not want to see; but at the same time, beyond the horror he reveals, he destroys the spells by which we are bound, destroys even the spell of horror itself. In Kafka, the tragic and the comic, contrary to the old French Classical doctrine,* are intimately intermingled. Each of the two elements is as true, as profound, as revealing as the other. They are the truth of life itself, as art must openly take that truth unto itself in complete clarity of consciousness.

In this respect there is a remarkable analogy between the art of Kafka and that of Chaplin. But while the Chaplinesque clown provokes laughter at first and only suggests little by little the depth of human misery, with Kafka the misery is first made obvious and only then does laughter rise up as a liberating force. How great is that liberating force? Is it only stoic and ephemeral, or does it really suggest the dawn of hope? This question must be answered in order to arrive at the final significance of Kafka's work.

---

* French seventeenth-century Classical literary doctrine forbade the introduction of comic elements into "noble" genres such as dramatic tragedy and the epic [trans. note].

Interpreters of his work have seen everything in it. There are, of course, the direct meanings: *The Judgment* is the struggle of the son against the father; *The Castle*, the epic of the unemployed; *The Trial*, an indictment of the atrocious incoherence of human justice; *The Metamorphosis*, the drama of illness, etc. But behind these obvious meanings other hidden meanings can be uncovered. *The Castle* is also a recasting of the myth of the Wandering Jew, of the Jews' inability to settle and to become assimilated in the countries to which they have migrated. *The Trial* hides, under the judicial ceremony, the anguish of a sick man treated (or maltreated) and condemned to death by doctors. *The Castle* has also been interpreted as being symbolic of Kafka himself, incapable of marrying, caught up in futile travels; *The Trial*, as an evocation of modern witch hunts or, if one prefers, a parody on the theme of original sin. If one were to enumerate all of the interpretations that have been put forth, one after another, the list would be endless. They may appear plausible or absurd in turn, but it is their heterogeneous accumulation that is most surprising and that often gives an unfortunate impression of gratuitous incoherence, either on the part of Kafka himself or on the part of his commentators.

The question of interpretation is a major one, but it is continually obscured by false problems. For example, Marthe Robert, who has done some excellent French translations of Kafka's work, feels it necessary to write: "Treated as true symbols, Kafka's images are, in fact, open to so many opposing, contradictory, even irreconcilable meanings, that one must choose arbitrarily among them or accept them all in disregard for any coherence."*

Wishing at all cost to save coherence in Kafka, Marthe Robert can find no other way of doing so except to support the fantastic thesis that Kafka is an anti-symbolist. This position is based on the old confusion, forever discredited and forever reasserted, between symbolism and allegory.

Allegory, being artificial and intentionally prefabricated, can by definition have only one meaning—and this in exactly the

* Marthe Robert, *Kafka* (Paris: Gallimard, 1960), p. 112.

same way as a thesis novel. Once its intended meaning is ex-
tracted, allegory remains an empty shell.

The symbol, on the contrary, being alive and spontaneous,
goes beyond the author's intentions, even if he is partially aware
of what is coming to life within him. The symbol is a live force
of the imagination; it is loaded with a multiplicity and a plenitude of meanings so that it is never reducible to a single interpretation or even to any given number of interpretations. In
opposition to allegory, which represents a predetermined line
of thought that could have been formulated in other terms, the
symbol expresses directly that which could not have been expressed without it.*

Does this multiplicity of meanings produce an incoherent
spectacle? Certainly not. It merely reflects a multiplicity of
levels and perspectives that do not negate but complement one
another. They seem incoherent only insofar as one confuses
symbolism with allegory, whose two-dimensional flatness can
never represent more than one single pattern. The world of
symbols is like a volume of space that can contain an indefinite
quantity of figures. It is no more incoherent to recognize in
Kafka's work a plurality of sexual, familial, clinical, professional,
social, or religious implications than it is to ascertain the same
multiplicity of levels in Kafka's own life or in the life of a large
city, whether it be Prague or Paris. All of these levels, far from
being mutually exclusive, intertwine and interrelate endlessly.
The complex volume of a city, with its many thriving interrelationships, is similar to the complex volume of symbolism. If
one granted only one symbolic level to Kafka, his work would
be extremely impoverished thereby, for its inspired richness is
derived from the multitude of implications that it contains, from
its multiplicity of levels, perspectives, and interrelationships. In
Kafka there is no single polarity, no uniformity, no reduction

* Cf. Brod, *FK*, p. 193. Scholem, *op. cit.*, p. 22–25. Jean Baruzi, *Saint
Jean de la Croix et le problème de l'expérience mystique*. Marcel Ray-
mond, *De Baudelaire au Surréalisme*. Corbin, *Avicenne et le récit vision-
naire*, etc.

to a common denominator, but the oceanic movement of life. One must plunge into it; there is no other way in.

The first major difficulty might well be discovering the final significance inherent in each series of symbols. Thus one may wonder if the social symbolism in Kafka inspires or denies revolt. By the same token, does the sexual and familial symbolism suggest rejection of the institution of marriage or an apology for it? We have already seen the profound ambiguity of Kafka's symbolism. One cannot answer these questions with oversimplifications, as if one were dealing with an allegory. Yet this same question must now be posed with regard to religious symbolism in Kafka.

Here one must mention a second major difficulty, that of knowing how the various series of symbols are composed. They certainly form a whole, bound together by the coherence of life itself, but can one find in them a definite polarization, and, if so, what is it? Is Kafka's religious symbolism only one other aspect of his work buried among many others, or does it actually provide us with the key to the ultimate significance of his thought? There is the great problem that remains to be examined.

How can we cut directly to the heart of such a question? On the one hand, we have seen the rebirth of Judaism in Kafka's life. On the other hand, there is the oppressive and despairing aspect of his work. Is there some footbridge over the abyss that separates these two sides of the Kafkean universe?

If one goes first to the work, one can ascertain by examining it closely that there do exist at least some signs of hope, however fleeting or strange they may seem.

The Trial ends with the execution of K., but at that very moment a light flashes from a window in the top story of a nearby house:

Who was it? A friend? A good man? Someone who sympathized? Someone who wanted to help? Was it one person only? Or was it mankind? Was help at hand? Were there arguments in his favor that had been overlooked? Of course there must be. Logic is doubtless unshakable, but it cannot withstand a man who wants to go on living. Where was the Judge whom he had never seen? Where was the High Court, to which he had never penetrated? (*The Trial*, p. 286).

From the point of view of any line of logic that is applicable only to the life this side of death (i.e. life itself, as we know it), all of this means nothing, since K. is about to die. But what does the passage tell us about Kafka?

Let us consider *The Penal Colony*. Once the officer is dead, having committed suicide on the torture machine, the explorer heads back toward the harbor. On the way he is shown the tomb of the former Commandant on which he reads the old prophecy: ". . . After a certain number of years the Commandant will rise again . . . Have faith and wait!" (*The Penal Colony*, p. 226). Have faith, await the resurrection. Behind these words looms the horizon of the Jewish faith. Death is not the end of everything.

In the same way, the sinister mockery of *The Metamorphosis* and of *Investigations of a Dog* reveals an obsession with something that goes beyond the immediate suffering of this life. In *The Penal Colony* the condemned man always ends by spitting out the rice pap that is offered him, for he now waits only for the ecstasy that will come at the end of the torture. Gregor Samsa is repelled by any kind of food—even by milk, which he loved:

"I'm hungry enough," said Gregor sadly to himself, "but not for that kind of food."*

The "dog" also discovers something beyond material life:

The science of music, if I am correctly informed, is perhaps still more comprehensive than that of nurture . . . A border region between these two sciences . . . had already attracted my attention. I mean the theory of incantation, by which food is called down.**

---

* "The Metamorphosis," in *The Penal Colony*, p. 119.
** "Investigations of a Dog," in *The Great Wall of China*, trans. Willa and Edwin Muir (New York: Schocken, 1946), pp. 76–77.

For his part, Gregor Samsa listens so avidly to his sister's violin that he feels, beyond the mere pleasure of hearing the music, that he may be discovering a way of attaining the impossible:

Was he an animal, that music had such an effect upon him? He felt as if the way were opening before him to the unknown nourishment he craved.*

The great final feast in *Amerika*, at which food in distributed in profusion while wine flows freely and thousands of golden trumpets sound exultantly, is not then an isolated vision, but a naïve apotheosis of music and food transfigured by the magic of the feast. All personal differences aside, there is a striking analogy between the threefold importance of food, music, and feasting in Kafka and the threefold importance of the *madeleine*, the Vinteuil sonata, and the fête at the Hôtel de Guermantes in Proust's *À la recherche du temps perdu:* these are flashes of revelation of another life in this life itself.

No less important in Kafka is the theme of the window. It conceals, in fact, multiple implications; here, however, we will consider particularly—in comparison with the suddenly illuminated window above the street near K.'s place of execution—the window that is illuminated by the dawn at the moment of Gregor Samsa's death in his room. Is this nothing more than a sudden burst of flame just before the descent into nothingness, or is it rather an annunciation, the dawn of another life, the first spark of a whole world of light? Is it there that the true Judge, the true Lord of the Castle, the true Emperor of China resides?

And through the window the reflected splendors of divine worlds fell on the hands of the leaders . . .**

Do all these symbolic figures, inaccessible in this world, represent someone who is finally real and accessible, someone who will render true justice, provide the true dwelling place, and change all suffering into joy? Is death an end or a new beginning?

* "The Metamorphosis," p. 121.
** *The Great Wall of China*, p. 157.

But first of all, is there an afterlife for Kafka? On this point there is no doubt: "My life here is just as if I were quite certain of a second life . . . ," he declared (*DI*, 46). In his work, moreover, there actually exists an afterlife. The "Mausoleum Guard" can tell us something about it. Posted as a sentinel at that imperial crypt that is "the boundary between the human world and the other,"* every night he undergoes the assault of the dead:

. . . Out, all of them want to get out. After midnight you can see all the hosts from the tomb gathered around my house. I think that if they were not so closely crowded together, they would all come in together through the narrow crack in my window, with all that they are (*Ibid.*, 295).

This time the theme of the window is again linked to that of death, but here, it is from the dead that the initiative comes.

In the sketch, "I Was a Visitor among the Dead," we find a further development of the theme of the crypt beyond the tomb. The visitor converses with a young girl who shows him her coffin and a discarded length of cloth: " 'This is my shroud,' she said, 'but I don't wear it' " (*DF*, 232).

The "hunter Gracchus" is more explicit, but his story is even more strange, if that is possible. At Riva, where he is received by the burgomaster, he admits that he has been dead for some years but is still alive "In a certain sense."

"My death ship lost its way; a wrong turn of the wheel, a moment's absence of mind on the pilot's part, a longing to turn aside towards my lovely native country, I cannot tell what it was; I only know this, that I remained on earth and that ever since my ship has sailed earthly waters. So I, who asked for nothing better than to live among my mountains, travel after my death through all the lands of the earth."

* "Der Gruftwächter," in *Gessamelte Schriften,* V, ed. Max Brod, (New York: Schocken, 1936), p. 290. So far as I have been able to ascertain, this dramatic sketch has not been translated into English. The passage cited here is my own translation, which Professor Eugene Dobson of the German department of the University of Alabama was kind enough to verify [trans. note].

"And you have no part in the other world? asked the Burgomaster, knitting his brow.

"I am for ever," replied the hunter, "on the great stair that leads up to it. On that infinitely wide and spacious stair I clamber about . . . But when I make a supreme flight and see the gate shining before me, I awaken presently on my old ship. The fundamental error of my onetime death grins at me as I lie in my cabin . . ."*

Why does Kafka return thus in so many different ways to ancient themes from tales evoking the survival of the dead in a form scarcely different from the existence of the living? In his fictional universe, in any case, the executions in *The Judgment, The Trial, The Metamorphosis,* and *The Penal Colony,* cannot be separated from the beginnings of another life. But what is the extent of that other life?

Several times in the course of Kafka's meditations one finds allusions to the Hindu and Platonic conceptions of the transmigration of souls, notably in the following passage:

Many shades of the departed are occupied solely in licking at the waves of the river of death because it flows from our direction and still has the salty taste of our seas. Then the river rears back in disgust, the current flows the opposite way and brings the dead drifting back into life. But they are happy, sing songs of thanksgiving, and stroke the indignant waters (*DF*, 34).

In this case, Kafka's revulsion is clearly discernible through the attraction held for him by the myth of transmigration. Elsewhere he expresses it in a still more precise manner:

One of the first signs of the beginnings of understanding is the wish to die. This life appears unbearable, another unattainable. One is no longer ashamed of wanting to die; one asks to be moved from the old cell, which one hates, to a new one, which one will only in time come to hate. In this there is also a residue of belief that during the move the master will chance to come along the corridor, look at the prisoner and say: "This man is not to be locked up again. He is to come to me" (*DF*, 35).

The allusion is clear; beyond the interminable cycles of wandering, of ghosts or of reincarnated beings, man thirsts for

* "The Hunter Gracchus," in *The Great Wall of China,* pp. 210–11.

something else. Kafka's mythology makes this clearer than any theory. Such extensions of life would be an infinite repetition of events like those in *The Castle* and *The Trial*. The impossibility of entering the castle, of obtaining justice, the torture of "endless postponement," would no longer come only once to overwhelm man in the course of a single life; they would track him indefinitely. Then *The Castle* and *The Trial* would have neither beginning nor end; they would each represent nothing more than another revolution of the wheel in an endless cycle. They would take on the proportions of a monstrous cosmogonic myth of "becoming" placed under the sign of "endless postponement"—truly the torture of Sisyphus for all eternity.

7

The Most
Unbridled Individualism
in Faith

Kafka was not and had no wish to be Sisyphus.

Our salvation is death, but not this one (*DF*, 101).

There must then be a true resolution, a true death where "the gate to on high" is accessible, where the master comes to liberate the captive, a death that gives access to the true "castle" of transcendence.

But of what value was the "remnant of faith" that inspired such a hope? Does not such another life defy the imagination?

Wonderful, entirely self-contradictory idea that someone who died at 3 A.M.,* for instance, immediately thereafter, about dawn enters into a higher life. What incompatibility there is between the visibly human and everything else! How out of one mystery there always comes a greater one! In the first moment the breath leaves the human calculator (*DI*, 317).

Not only do we lack the necessary images, we lack even the words that would be needed to impart substance to life incommensurate with ours. All legends that deal with life beyond the tomb, including those of Kafka, are only traps. Since we cannot imagine the other life except by means of images drawn from life as we know it, the essence of the other ultimately eludes us. Lan-

* A direct allusion to Gregor Samsa's death.

guage, in any case, fails when it attempts to describe that other life:

For everything outside the phenomenal world, language can only be used allusively, but never even approximately in a comparative way, since, corresponding as it does to the phenomenal world, it is concerned only with property and its relations (DF, 40).

We know the properties of things accessible to the senses; we can analyze and compare them in many ways. But how can we compare them with the properties of a life that is invisible and radically superior to ours? There is no way. The language of realism, by its very nature, fails in the attempt. One may sometimes suppose that the language of symbolism can succeed through analogy, but this is possible only to the extent that the other life resembles ours, while that which is peculiar to it—the qualities in which it differs totally from the life we know—is absolutely indescribable. Some place more faith in the abstract language of philosophy—theological or otherwise—but the same limits inexorably impose themselves.

Kafka certainly does not conclude that language is thus reduced to complete powerlessness. Rather he concludes that language, whether abstract or symbolic, having departed from the realm of its own inherent qualities, can speak only by means of allusions. One wonders, then, which is the more astonishing, the weakness inherent in the power of symbolic language or its fantastic ambition.

It is through the inexpressible fragment of the unknowable, deep in himself, that man can communicate "by allusion" with the universal sphere of the unknowable.

But how? Buddhism, the ultimate in human mysticism, can speak of Nirvana in negative terms only, for Buddhist transcendance is totally inexpressible. But Kafka was deeply imbued with the spirit of Judaism, and the basis of Judaism is revelation, that is to say, by definition the interrelationship of the divine Word and human utterance. However, revelation itself does not reveal what death alone can lay bare; it delivers the divine utterance within the limits of human utterance. It can reveal the secret of life hereafter only in an allusive manner.

In speaking of Abraham, Kafka was led to men
and to remark: "The oracle is never equivocal'
What he says, in effect, is that even the great orac\
the Bible conceals for him a fundamental ambiguity
affronts that ambiguity with a violence perhaps wit

The way in which he comments on Moses is even more unusual, for he does it from the point of view of his own meditation upon death:

Anyone who has once been in a state of suspended animation can
tell terrible stories about it, but he cannot say what it is like after
death, he has actually been no nearer to death than anyone else,
fundamentally he has only "lived" through an extraordinary experience . . . For instance, Moses certainly experienced something extraordinary on Mount Sinai, but instead of submitting to this extraordinary experience . . . he fled down the mountain . . . From
both, however, from those who have returned from a state of suspended animation and from Moses, who returned, one can learn a
great deal, but the decisive thing cannot be discovered from them,
for they have not discovered [it]. If they had . . . , they would not
have come back at all (DF, 392).

This passage clarifies the reason, according to Kafka, that the
first sign of the beginning of consciousness is the desire to die:
the only gateway to true knowledge is death, since death is the
gateway to true life.

Certainly the gateway itself is hideous enough, but it suggests
nothing of what is hidden behind it. The two notions of death
are disjointed. Rereading The Metamorphosis in the light of the
passage cited above, which begins "Wonderful, entirely self-
contradictory idea . . . ," we can now comprehend that in truth
there is—unfortunately—nothing fantastic or inconceivable in
the idea that a man can be transformed into a vermin. Far from
being a strange case, it conforms to the universal law in the same
way as Baudelaire's "charogne."* The only anomaly in Kafka's
tale is in the fact that the vermin phase is anticipated. Instead of

* In "Une Charogne" (Les fleurs du mal), Baudelaire tells his still
young and beautiful beloved that after death she, like all creatures of this
world, will resemble the rotting, vermin-ridden corpse of an animal that
they have encountered during the course of a walk [trans. note].

being posterior to death and waiting for the grave, the metamorphosis begins with illness and, step by step, in complete
evidence, accompanies the progress of the agony. This simultaneity alone may seem fantastic. It is, however, a thousand
times less fantastic than that other simultaneity which follows
the universal law: it is at the very moment of death that man
becomes on the one hand a vermin and on the other a butterfly.

Abject and sublime, oppressive and liberating, death is the
greatest scandal of the human condition. Why does evil exist
in all its forms: sickness, sin, death—and uncertainty as to what
lies beyond death? Kafka raised this question and answered it
in that calm, hard tone typical of him:

We are nihilistic thoughts that came into God's head (*FK*, 75).

Brod, upon hearing these words, wished to investigate their
meaning further: "I quoted in support the doctrine of the Gnos-
tics concerning the Demiurge, the evil creator of the world, the
doctrine of the world as a sin of God's. 'No,' said Kafka, 'I
believe we are not such a radical relapse of God's, only one of
his bad moods. He had a bad day.' 'So there would be hope
outside our world?' He smiled, 'Plenty of hope—for God—no
end of hope—only not for us'" (*FK*, 75).

This is faith—faith without hope or charity it is true, but
nevertheless faith that returns obstinately to the biblical oracle
in order to consult and to interpret it endlessly.

What drew Kafka's attention above all was the beginning of
Genesis, especially the Paradise episode, the very prime source
of the oracular revelation. Of all archaic myths explaining human origins this is the only one that has passed beyond the
folklore of its native land to be spread throughout the world
by the triple force of Judaism, Christianity, and Islam. No other
concentrates so strongly in its structure the link between life,
guilt, death, and salvation; the tragic interrelationship of the
human and the divine, of immanence and transcendence. In one
sense the reply of Genesis is categorical: Paradise was only life
and happiness. Death was not the Law of Paradise. After all the

disaster of evil, unhappiness, and death in human history, the resurrection is no more than the reestablishment of the Law of Paradise. This is the fundamental reply of the oracle concerning the mystery of human life.

But the manner in which the oracle resolves the mystery is in itself still an enigma. It is enigmatic by its very formulation in a symbolic account, and the more so in that its reply elicits new questions from mankind and new, similarly enigmatic and allusive replies from the oracle. Why has the Law of Paradise been suspended throughout the duration of historical time? Because of Original Sin? But what is Original Sin, how could it have intruded in Paradise, how could God have permitted it to occur—and why?

This is the gordian knot, the kernel of darkness that cannot be broken open. To these questions Kafka made a double reply. On the one hand he wrote:

The original sin, the ancient wrong committed by man, consists in the complaint, which man makes and never ceases making, that a wrong has been done to him, that the original sin was once committed upon him.*

On the other hand, men are free beings. Their very unhappiness is the most evident proof of it:

The Fall is the proof of their freedom (*CWK*, 65).

Having plunged into the tragic mystery of the human condition, Kafka, the man of today, contemplates face-to-face his alter ego, Adam, the original man, the father of all men. Kafka knew that Adam is the living testimonial to the existence of the mystery, but Adam's revelation is enclosed in its own mystery. A third of the message has been annihilated, another third is undecipherable, and the last third is so searing that man can hardly bring himself to contemplate its deciphered meaning.

Fascinated, Kafka constantly probed for the meaning of the message's symbols: Paradise, the two trees, the interdiction, the serpent, the transgression, the Fall (*DF*, 34 ff., 82, 85 ff.).

* "He," in *The Great Wall of China*, p. 270.

He left us only a very small number of his reflections—comet-like illuminations that flash for but a second or two. The unfathomable night is made no less thick for their brief appearances. Kafka's meditation on the relationship between consciousness and death redoubles the mystery and is summed up in this violent contradiction:

"If _____, thou shalt die"* means: knowledge of Good and Evil is both a step leading to eternal life and an obstacle in the way (*DF*, 88).

Man was made in the image and likeness of God, but that resemblance could not develop to its highest degree except in freedom and in the knowledge of all the power implicit in that freedom. The choice of entering into the abyss of divine love or into the abyss of a total break with God are the two antinomical and indissociable faces of mankind's vertiginous freedom. This is the fundamental temptation of Genesis, repeated in each moment of historical time until the very end of the world.

From where then can salvation come? From the Messiah promised to Israel? Here again Kafka's attitude is typical. He does not impugn that promise. He does not reject the coming of the Messiah. But when Janouch questioned him about the fact that Christians recognized Christ as the Messiah and reproached the Jews for not having done the same, Kafka exclaimed: "Perhaps that is really so . . . But what a cruel God it is who makes it possible for his creatures not to recognize him" (*CWK*, 70). The ambiguity of Genesis is not due to its archaic nature; the Gospel is also an ambiguous message, not in its content but in its presentation. Is it the message of the King? Its style is royal, but the King's seal is not visibly affixed to the message. The resurrection, however, is the King's seal, but this event took place in the margin of history: it goes beyond the limits of private life, it is public and spectacular, but it was not graven imperatively

---

* A reference to Genesis 2:17: "But of the tree of the knowledge of good and evil thou shalt not eat, for in the day that thou eatest of it thou shalt die" [trans. note].

into the official facts of history. Divine ambiguity and human freedom are inexorably bound together. If not, it is the end of history. This seemed so true to Kafka that when he thought of the future coming of the Judaic Messiah, he declared:

The Messiah will come only when he is no longer necessary, he will come only one day after his arrival, he will not come on the last day, but on the last day of all (*DF*, 78).

Which means:

The Messiah will come . . . when the graves open (*DF*, 78).

In effect, then, the Messiah is no longer a messenger. He only records the end of the world. Thus He does not enter into history in order to change it, to transform it in the course of its development.

Thus Kafka's position seems singular: on the one hand he does not deny the royal origin of the biblical message as atheists or followers of non-Mosaic religions do, but neither does he accept this message as it stands. He questions it, not in the name of a system, but personally. It is Kafka alone, as Kafka, who enters into a dispute with God.

In the fragment in which he declares, "The Messiah will come . . . when the graves open," he inserts between these words this strange statement:

The Messiah will come as soon as the most unbridled individualism is possible in faith . . . (*DF*, 78).

The most unbridled individualism in faith is his idea, his expectation, his conviction, and, already, his conscious and obstinate endeavor. For he did not intend to await the end of the world in order to know the individual nature of his eternal destiny; it was in this life, *hic et nunc*, that he intended to practice it. In the biblical revelation, from Genesis to the eschatology of the prophets, he recognized the universal destiny of humanity, but for himself he admitted neither common knowledge nor common destiny.

Was Kafka not speaking of himself personally when he wrote:

He is a free and secure citizen of this earth, for he is attached to a chain that is long enough to make all areas of the earth accessible to him, and yet only so long that nothing can pull him over the edges of the earth. At the same time, however, he is also a free and secure citizen of heaven, for he is also attached to a similarly calculated heavenly chain. Thus, if he wants to get into heaven, he is choked by the earthly one. And in spite of this he has all the possibilities, and feels that it is so; indeed, he even refuses to attribute the whole thing to a mistake in the original chaining (*DF*, 41).

Despite the double chain, Kafka rejects original sin and claims even to have "all the possibilities." But how? By what right? Even Moses, greatest of the Old Testament prophets, was riven by these two chains; he was able to find the way to Canaan but he could not enter, simply because his was a human life; on Sinai he had walked all about the edge of the abyss of death, but he had not descended into it else he would not have been able to return. What more can one hope?

But the Bible conceals more than one mystery. Following some remarks concerning Genesis, Kafka wrote this sibylline sentence:

And Enoch walked with God, and he was not; for God took him (*DII*, 156).*

This is a direct allusion to the well known passage from Scripture: "Enoch walked with God, and he was not; for God

---

* There is a discrepancy in the *Journal Intime*, Marthe Robert's translation of Kafka's *Tagebücher (Diaries)*. Kafka's original German reads: "Und dieweil er ein göttlich Leben führte, nahm ihn Gott hinweg und ward nicht mehr gesehen," the exact German version of Genesis 5:24. Instead of translating this by the French biblical equivalent, "Enoch marcha avec Dieu, puis il disparut, car Dieu l'enleva," Robert translated Kafka's German quotation (which was not within quotation marks) as a paraphrase of the actual biblical passage: "Et comme il menait une vie divine, Dieu le prit avec lui et on ne le vit plus" (p. 467), *i.e.*: "And as he led a holy life, God took him with Him and he was seen no more." This confusion accounts for Carrouges' characterizing this sentence from the *Diaries* as "sibylline." I have cited the English biblical passages as given in Martin Greenberg's and Hannah Arendt's English translation. Cf. *Tagebücher* (New York: Schocken, 1948), p. 502. [trans. note].

took him" (Genesis 5:24). According to the tradition born of this passage, Enoch, before Elias (II Kings 2:11), was carried up into heaven without undergoing death. The prophets would then have in fact lived out the normal immortality of Adam—despite original sin.

Could there be thus, somewhere, a "passage" from this world where one need not submit to the law of death that grew out of Original Sin and where the postponed arrival of the Messiah does not await the end of the world? And if this passage were within ourselves? Did not Enoch "walk with God" before disappearing from this world?

For Kafka that way existed, and it was nothing other than Paradise itself: "We were expelled from Paradise, but it was not destroyed" (*DF*, 85). This interpretation conforms strictly to the biblical message and, moreover, to Christian tradition. The idea that the terrestial Paradise still exists is quite uncommon in occidental countries today. It has never been either affirmed or condemned by the Church, but one finds numerous traces of it, notably in St. Ambrose, St. Isadore of Seville, and even in St. Thomas Aquinas. The idea was widespread during the Middle Ages (see Joinville's *Mémoires*, for example) up to the time of Columbus who, unintentionally, gave it the *coup de grâce* by discovering a continent—North America—that he was not looking for.

But Kafka was not some kind of mystical geographer; he was oriented in an entirely different direction, that of a singular conception of time, in which he seems to have been influenced by Kierkegaard. He was seeking the *permanent* relationship between man, even the man of today, and the original but indestructible Paradise. Being eternal, the expulsion of man from Paradise is in one sense final and ineluctable. But in another sense it was not an isolated act committed once and for all, but an event that is reiterated every moment for each of us. In this sense it is "possible not only that we might remain in Paradise permanently, but that we may in fact be there permanently . . ." (*DF*, 41).

If time is only "the eternal repetition of the process" (*Ibid.*), then Paradise is here, *hic et nunc*, as is the Fall. Our expulsion from Paradise would only be an expulsion of our consciousness from paradisiacal lucidity. It would suffice simply to invert the terms, whereupon it would be retroactively as though the Fall had never occurred—as though we were still in Paradise. What Borges was able to extract from this strange mythology is known,* while Kafka only skimmed the surface of the whole question. Even here one can speak only by way of allusion, for the sensual Paradise interferes with the spiritual one.

Kafka, moreover, was not much tempted to engage at length in great metaphysico–theological games. With him it was always more a question of a concrete search, of the search for that true "superior" life that is ordinarily accessible only through death. Since death can reveal its unbearable presence here on earth, that presence being a fact, why should that superior life not be accessible through some form of spiritual violence during this life itself?** It would be a matter, then, of rejecting the roundabout way of the Fall, death, and salvation, in order to claim a shorter way.

What is that shorter way? Kafka had a name for it: the reconquest of the *indestructible* that is hidden in ourselves.

* Jorge-Luis Borges (1899–   ), an Argentine writer and professor at the University of Buenos Aires. Some of the best of his highly original speculative metaphysical and literary essays are to be found in *A Personal Anthology*, ed. by Anthony Kerrigan (New York: Grove Press, Inc., 1967), *Ficciones*, trans. Anthony Kerrigan *et al.* (New York: Grove Press, Inc., 1962), and *Other Inquisitions*, trans. Ruth L. C. Simms (Austin: University of Texas Press, 1964). For passages of particular relevance to M. Carrouges' discussion here, see *Other Inquisitions*, pp. 21, 19–25, 76, 172–87 *passim* [trans. note].

** On this point—and on the questions of insomnia and gnosticism—we can only mention in passing how interesting it would be to make a detailed comparison between Kafka's position and that of Lautréamont. The new edition of Lautréamont's *Poésies* (edited by Georges Goldfayn and Gérard Legrand) that has recently been published (Editions Arcanes) makes a most remarkable contribution to this subject, insofar as the Montevidean is concerned. [The Comte de Lautréamont is of course the pseudonym of Isadore Ducasse (1846–1870), a French poet born in Montevideo, Uruguay. He is best known for his *Chants de Maldoror*. The Surrealists consider him one of their most eminent precursors (trans. note)].

8

Assault
on the Frontier
of the Absolute

For the Westerner, generally materialistic and dualistic in his outlook, the spiritual is a rather vague concept, relegated either to the realm of myth, in the pejorative sense of the word, or to some other realm more or less apart from everyday life. Kafka, however, declared unequivocally:

There is nothing but a spiritual world . . . (*DF*, 41).

This statement suggests to us that Kafka's strangeness does not derive solely from the more or less bizarre aspects of his imagery but, more especially, from a conception of the world whose singularity appears abrupt. For such a conception must not be confused either with idealism or with spiritualism. The foregoing affirmation in no way seeks to annihilate the reality of the sensual world, but to present it in an entirely unaccustomed light. Kafka, in fact, adds immediately:

. . . What we call the world of the senses is the Evil in the spiritual world, and what we call Evil is only the necessity of a moment in our eternal evolution (*DF*, 39).

He futher clarifies this statement by saying:

Evil is a radiation of the human consciousness in certain transitional positions. It is not actually the sensual world that is a mere appearance; what is so is the evil of it, which, admittedly, is what constitutes the sensual world in our eyes (*DF*, 43).

Thus, the sensual world is real for Kafka, but its reality exists only by virtue of the superior and universal reality of the spiritual world that encompasses everything. What constitutes pure appearance is evil, for it distorts our view of the sensual world, but it is only a pathological radiation of our consciousness in the state brought about by the Fall. At once spiritual and sensual, the true life is there; we have only to regain our self-possession in order to rediscover it.

The way of that true life is not distant; it is immediately available and open to all, in life and in faith in life.

"It cannot be said that we are lacking in faith. Even the simple fact of our life is of a faith-value that can never be exhausted." "You suggest there is some faith-value in this? One *cannot* not-live, after all." "It is precisely in the 'Cannot after all' that the mad strength of faith lies; it is in this negation that it takes on form" (*DF*, 48).

The determination with which men struggle together against everything that seeks to crush them—forces of nature, sickness, death—is the manifestation of a will to unconditional life that radiates from the depths of the human spirit. It provides the overflowing measure of man's faith in life.

It is useless to treat that faith as madness, as a vague desire, as an epiphenomenon. It is a fact, an act of life, and as such it is the immanent revelation that there is something in us that is unconditional and indestructible:

Believing means liberating the indestructible element in oneself, or, more accurately, being indestructible, or, more accurately, being (*DF*, 78).

That faith is not an irrelevant phenomenon; it is a direct manifestation of the self, or better, the principal manifestation of the infinite virtuality of our being. It signifies our consciousness of being an integral part of the Absolute. It is a universal fact for humanity:

The indestructible is one: it is each individual human being and, at the same time, it is common to all, hence the incomparably indivisible union that exists between human beings (*DF*, 42).

And it is an unconditional fact:

Man cannot live without a permanent trust in something indestructible in himself, though both the indestructible element and the trust may remain permanently hidden from him. One of the ways in which this hiddenness can express itself is through faith in a personal god (*DF*, 39).

This faith is distinctly different from religious faith. Faith in a personal god is only one aspect of the problem. The same goes for the faith that an atheist may have in the future of humanity and in the absolute reality of matter, or the faith of a Buddhist in Nirvana. Among these different types of belief, disagreement centers on the content, the object, the subject, or the ultimate end of the faith in question. Kafka's thought moves on another plane: that of *faith* purified by a radical phenomenological reduction to a pure fact that is lived by all men in the form of a decisive metaphysical experience. This is once again why he adds:

The fact that there is nothing but a spiritual world deprives us of hope and gives us certainty (*DF*, 41).

This faith has no other content than itself, and this is absolutely sufficient unto it. Far from being a vicious circle, it represents the end of the vicious circle in which we find ourselves. The dichotomy of faith as subject (man) and faith as object (the indestructible) is a mere transitory appearance. Faith is only the direct radiation of life. Born out of life's plenitude, it leads us back to that same plenitude. Thus faith reveals the very heart of the indestructible because it is only our awareness of our personal "indestructible." Faith seemed to be merely hope, but it is revealed as certainty; it seemed nostalgic for a lost Paradise, but it is revealed as a recovery of the indestructible.

Seemingly derived from the existential realm, it reveals to us that existence itself is only a surface appearance within the existential realm and is, in fact, the irreducible being of transcendence.

Departing from Judaic thought, modified by the Kabbala, by various theosophic and anthroposophic currents, but, above all, finally by his own unbridled individualistic reflection, Kafka's thought constitutes a new gnosis. On the basis of that gnosis he conceived a new yoga. Yet this relationship is reversible, for it was in spontaneously living this yoga that Kafka invented the gnosis.

But if a gnosis can be expressed in general terms, such terms are insufficient for a yoga that is by definition a concrete experience. Thus, one is particularly struck by certain signals that one comes across here and there in Kafka's diaries. In 1911, he recorded a conversation with a theosophist, Dr. Rudolph Steiner, in which he said:

I have, to be sure, experienced states (not many) which in my opinion correspond very closely to the clairvoyant states described by you, Herr Doktor, in which I completely dwelt in every idea, but also filled every idea, and in which I not only felt myself at my boundary, but at the boundary of the human in general (DI, 58).

More or less similar states of illumination subsequently appear again, such as those Kafka mentions with regard to the famous night in 1913 when he wrote *The Judgment* (DI, 275), and again during the writing of *The Giant Mole* in 1914 (DII, 105).

In spite of the similarity of his personal experiences with those of Steiner, the founder of "anthroposophy," Kafka was categorical in his rejection—out of fear of "confusion" (DI, 58) —of any esoteric doctrine that was not his own since that kind of mythology was for him only a diversion, a collection of fables, a diverting of his attention away from the radical nakedness of the indestructible.

On the other hand, states of illumination are not only rare and unstable, they are worth no more than the ransom one pays

for them and for the progressive development of the consciousness that is their by-product. They stand as signals along the
way, but they are not the way itself.

Born out of unbridled individualism, this personal yoga can
have had no other vital source than the turning inward of
Kafka's entire being during his youth. Having failed to find
expression in brutal, external revolt, his feelings of opposition
toward his father took the form of an internal rending asunder
that was of unprecedented violence.

There was no opposition between the progressive destruction
of Kafka's existence and his progress toward the indestructible.
There was, on the contrary, an indissoluble dialectical inter-
dependence. The division within Kafka continued to deepen
throughout the course of his broken engagements, the impossible
job, illness, his painful sense of social dislocation, his insomnia
and daydreams, the burning conflict between passion for Judaism and criticism of it. Kafka did not simply enter into a state of
solitude, nor were his reactions to his situation limited to a mere
change of outlook. At the very depths of his being the vital
structures that ordinarily integrate the social self into the world
around it collapsed, resulting in the exposure of the entire being.
Kafka found himself not only a stranger to others, but a stranger
to himself. He remained face to face with the only thing that
was left untouched and indestructible: his pure reality of being.

In 1921, ten years after his conversation with Steiner, he
wrote:

It is astounding how I have systematically destroyed myself in the
course of the years, it was like a slowly widening breach in a dam,
a purposeful action. The spirit that brought it about must now be
celebrating triumphs; why doesn't it let me take part in them? But
perhaps it hasn't yet achieved its purpose and can therefore think
of nothing else (*DII*, 195).

The very next day he replied:

It is entirely conceivable that life's splendor forever lies in wait
about each one of us in all its fulness, but veiled from view, deep
down, invisible, far off. It *is* there, though, not hostile, not reluctant,

not deaf. If you summon it by the right word, by its right name, it
will come. This is the essence of magic, which does not create but
summons (*Ibid.*).

The parallelism with life hidden behind death is striking. One
need only recall the death of Gregor Samsa: it is his transmutation into a vermin that leads to his eventual transmutation into
a butterfly. The ultimate degradation of the appearances of
being causes Gregor to enter into a superior form of life. His
destruction reintegrates him into the indestructible. Here we are
dealing with an imitation of death; a relative and progressive
destruction painfully frees the spirit and permits it to turn
slowly toward the splendor of hidden life. This is the period of
apprenticeship. With the passing of time and Kafka's last years,
this tragic apprenticeship was prolonged all the more.

We have already noted the appearance in Kafka's diary of a
fragment, dated January, 1922, in which he declares that he is in
a state of total collapse: ". . . Impossible to sleep, impossible to
stay awake, impossible to endure life, or, more exactly, the
course of life" (*DII*, 202). This final phrase is characteristic;
Kafka in no way condemns life itself, only its outward appearances.

In one sense this collapse was a ruinous, even catastrophic
experience. But in another sense it was a prodigious adventure,
the tragic and voluntary odyssey of liberation that opened the
way towards the unknown, as the rest of the passage indicates:

*This pursuit, originating in the midst of men, carries one in a direc-
tion away from them* [my italics]. The solitude that for the most
part has been forced on me, in part voluntarily sought by me—but
what was this if not compulsion too?—is now losing all its ambiguity
and approaches its denouement. Where is it leading? The strongest
likelihood is, that it may lead to madness; there is nothing more to
say, the pursuit goes right through me and rends me asunder. Or I
can—can I?—manage to keep my feet somewhat and be carried
along in the wild pursuit. Where, then, shall I be brought? "Pursuit," indeed, is only a metaphor. I can also say, "assault on the last
earthly frontier," an assault, moreover, launched from below, from

mankind, and since this too is a metaphor,* I can replace it by the metaphor of an assault from above, aimed at me from above. *All such writing is an assault on the frontiers; if Zionism had not intervened, it might easily have developed into a new secret doctrine, a Kabbalah. There are intimations of this. Though of course it would require a genius of an unimaginable kind to strike root again in the old centuries, or create the old centuries anew and not spend itself withal, but only then begin to flower forth* [my italics] (*DII*, 202–203).

This brilliant page must be read and reread. The phrase "carries one in a direction away from them [human beings]," is complementary to that of 1911 when he remarked to Rudolf Steiner that he felt himself "at the boundary of the human." The 1911 entry alludes only to states of illumination; the later entry, written after eleven long years during which the probing had become increasingly vast and deep, alludes to a state that has become generalized and permanent, not through the inevitably unstable process of illumination, but rather through a sort of cold, black light that sweeps an immense expanse of desert. What incredible stubbornness in that pursuit! But if this constitutes a yoga, or an attempt to attain a yoga, Kafka was far from posing as a yogi. He remained miraculously human at the very heart of that plunge into the depths of the inhuman. Not the singular ascesis that paralyzed him, not the hard pilgrimage towards the indestructible, not the sufferings that he endured— none of these dehumanized him. Kafka remained always Kafka. Or let us say that he remained the Franz Kafka of his childhood, for if all the bridges to the outside world were cut off, at the same time, the link between him and his childhood was never broken. One can see here how his passion for literature places him at the antipodes of the entertainers and mandarins for whom literature is only a game, a decorative art, a commodity—in short, an alien object that one man can produce as well as any other. For him, as for every true writer, literature is of course an object, but not a simple object; it is at the same time an ex-

---

* This entire passage shows to what extent Kafka was remarkably aware of the dialectical character of the contradictions inherent in symbolism.

ternal projection of his alter ego, of his *Doppelgänger*, of his second life, inseparable from the first.

Kafka's tales, thus, do not derive from the genre of the novel any more than they do from allegorical structures. They possess a peculiarly autobiographical value. Not that they are a sort of autobiography disguised in fable form. On the contrary, they express what an ordinary, "objective" autobiography can never express, the *personal* vision of one man. They are intensely realistic tales since all that Kafka's life enveloped (the material, familial, social, and collective aspects of his existence) are found in them in the form of the various contents, but every one of these contents is henceforth clearly discernible when viewed from Kafka's own personal point of view. In these tales there has taken place a complete fusion of the dreams and the tangible realities of his life. By way of these, the incommunicable becomes communicable. In a series of almost fable-like experiences he makes it possible for us to see the trajectory of his personal adventure, the curve of his own destiny.

Kafka's works should be reread in this axial light. It then becomes apparent that they provide us with more than a static representation expressing the author's resignation to the misery of his life. Rather they trace the dynamic movement, the slow and modest passage of the apprentice through the trials of initiation. And everyone knows, or should, that the value of an initiation is in direct proportion to the difficulty of its trials. They must be interminable if the initiation is to have a radical effect; they must literally devour life. In the extreme, no true process of initiation is completed except at the end of a lifetime of trials and combat, through the illumination of death. This point of view can only be derisive for those who believe that death is the end of everything, but the exact opposite was true for Kafka, since death, true death, was itself the very means of attaining the indestructible and of passing not only from hope to certainty, but from certainty to the possession of the indestructible.

In this light the tales of death contained in Kafka's work

take on a radically new meaning that in no way detracts from the old one, but that retroactively encompasses it.

When one has grasped the determining importance of death as condemnation and suicide in *The Judgment*, *The Penal Colony*, and *The Trial*, one has only begun to see from Kafka's own perspective. But one must take careful note of the fact that the suicide in *The Judgment* is voluntary, that the condemned man in *The Trial* personally leads the executioners to the place of execution without making any attempt to flee, that the officer in *The Penal Colony* voluntarily substitutes himself for the condemned man. Thus, what passed at first for final resignation to a death sentence is revealed as a willing desire to confront the decisive trial on the path to absolute liberation. In the same way, the promises that the hero of *The Castle* was to have received on his deathbed, far from being an example of supreme irony, meant to him that death alone opens the threshold of the "castle." Again, Gregor Samsa's sinister metamorphosis and the three chimes of the tower clock at dawn announce, to him, entry into a superior life.

Numerically speaking, the greater part of the symbolic content of these tales is filled with analogies related to trials we suffer in the physical world, but these analogies suggest precisely the path towards and not the way out of the adventure. Relatively few words are devoted to the symbolic representation of the way out, and these few are woven only of allusions, because all that touches upon death and the spiritual world defies representation. Kafka was not one to pose as a "living free spirit"; neither did he pretend to compete with those "visionaries" who suppose that their spiritual insight can anticipate the experience of death. To evoke for just an instant, in a few allusive lines, the marvel of what is beyond all that is tangible and mortal—that was the most he attempted to undertake. It is not by chance, therefore, that his longer tales are unfinished—not through any lack of belief in the indestructible but because it was at that very point that Kafka came up abruptly against the sheer wall of the unexplored and the inexpressible.

There Kafka's odyssey reached its ultimate limit between the natural world of men and the domain of the indestructible—in the wilderness.

Once again—in January, 1922—Kafka was to try to attain from a different angle a total knowledge of the trajectory of his destiny:

... Why did I want to quit the world? Because "he" [Kafka's father] would not let me live in it, in his world. Though indeed I should not judge the matter so precisely, for I am *now a citizen of this other world, whose relationship to the ordinary one is the relationship of the wilderness to cultivated land* [my italics] (I have been forty years wandering from Canaan); I look back at it like a foreigner, though in this other world as well—it is the paternal heritage I carry with me—I am the most insignificant and timid of all creatures and am able to keep alive thanks only to the special nature of its arrangements; in this world it is possible even for the humblest to be raised to the heights as if with lightning speed, though they can also be crushed forever as if by the weight of the seas. Should I not be thankful despite everything? Was it certain that I should find my way to this world? Could not "banishment" from one side,* coming together with rejection from this, have crushed me at the border? Is not Father's power such that nothing (not I, certainly) could have resisted his decree? It is indeed a kind of Wandering in the Wilderness in reverse that I am undergoing: I think that I am continually skirting the wilderness and am full of childish hopes (particularly as regards women) that "perhaps I shall keep in Canaan after all"—when all the while I have been decades in the wilderness and at those times when I am the wretchedest of creatures in the desert too, and *Canaan is perforce my only Promised Land, for no third place exists for mankind* [my italics] (*DII*, 213–14).

Everything is bound together. Without Hermann, no Franz; without an intolerable Hermann, no unconquerable Franz traveling off the beaten path into unexplored regions. And always that marvelous tone of simplicity and humanity. Kafka derived no pride or grandiloquence from his great adventure; he remained humble and as though completely disarmed.

---

* A "banishment" inflicted on every human being by the powers from above.

But what does that strange turning back to the theme of Canaan mean? Had not Judaism and Zionism set out on the road back to Canaan? How could Kafka have dreamed of taking the opposite way? Because once again opposites are equally true and inseparable. In one sense, the indestructible is the quintessence of Canaan, but the yoga that leads to the indestructible itself cannot be Canaan—or Paradise—since it is not a place that "exists for mankind." The purely spiritual world, detached from the physical, is not an inhabitable place. Kafka was no Buddhist, and did not stop at some kind of Nirvana as though having reached some absolute end. The physical is also an integral part of the Absolute. Like the "former Commandant," Kafka must rise again in order to find absolute liberation. There are only two—not three—possible dwelling places: the world of this life and the world of perfect restoration of all life at the end of this world and the beginning of the other.

Canaan, the land promised to Israel, was Kafka's "only Promised Land." While awaiting it, he lived in the wilderness during that year, 1922.

9

At the Dawn of Death, Love

Along the road to destruction, Kafka's life followed its inexorable course towards the indestructible—and also straight ahead towards the sanatorium at Kierling where he was to pass over the threshold of death.

But when death approaches in Kafka's novels, the windows are haloed with signs of hope. In his life, too, a sudden, prodigious leap enabled him to cross over the barriers of the impossible with lightning rapidity.

In July, 1923, Kafka and one of his sisters and her children went on a holiday to the beach at Graal-Müritz, on the Baltic shore. There he met by chance the members of a vacation colony from the Berlin Jewish People's Home in which he had shown such a keen interest a few years before. He began to frequent the members of the Home who had come to the colony that summer, and became acquainted with the new volunteer helpers.

Once he notices a girl in the Home's kitchen. She is busy scaling fish. "Such gentle hands, and such bloody work," he said with disapproval. The girl was ashamed, and had some other work allotted to her (*FK*, 196).

It was love. An immense and dazzling love. After so many years of impossible engagements, endless postponements, vain attempts to free himself from his father's domination, years of reckless immersion in the depths of solitude, there was an explosion of happiness.

That summer he was to reach his fortieth year, she her nineteenth or twentieth. Her name was Dora Dymant. A member of a "very much looked-up-to Polish Orthodox Jewish family," she had not been able, in spite of her love for her family, to endure the narrow constraints of the Orthodox tradition and she had escaped from the little Polish town where she had lived to come make her way alone in Germany. She was a remarkable student of Hebrew, and one of Franz's first conversations with her ended "in Dora's reading aloud a chapter from Isaiah in the original Hebrew" (FK, 196–97).

The impact of their meeting was irresistible. Kafka abandoned himself entirely to his love and drew from it an energy that he never knew he had. The vacation over, he returned to Prague only in order to break his chains once and for all. In a few weeks, in spite of his family's objections, he resigned his job, and moved out. In September he went to join Dora in Berlin. All of this happened with mad rapidity, and it should be noted that, in much the same way, the series of endless postponements in Kafka's novels are followed by lightning-quick actions.

If Kafka was able so joyfully to break through all the external obstacles, was it not first of all because in the warmth of Dora's love all inner obstacles melted like snow in bright sunlight? All his visions of marriage as a martyrdom and of the sexual union as punishment for happiness were dissipated within a few days, as if he had passed through and beyond a mirage.

Max Brod reported that Franz' life with Dora continued to be so harmonious that:

From Berlin he wrote to me for the first time that he felt happy, and that he was even sleeping well—an unheard-of novelty in these last years (FK, 197).

Unheard-of but quite logical. Was not all that had torn Kafka's life asunder solely and precisely his power of self-devastation? Was it not he himself who had drained off his own life's

substance in the insomnia of wakeful dreams, plunging himself
into a completely alien world where he might escape the tyrannical image of his father? But now love had exorcised the father,
had broken the father's subterranean power deep within Franz'
spirit. Through the power of woman Kafka had found his life's
happiness. He had seized Ariadne's thread, which always led
Theseus to victory over the perils of the Labyrinth and over the
Minotaur himself.

Some will undoubtedly consider it shocking that Kafka
should have thus set up housekeeping with a very young girl.
In some cases such an incident would perhaps be shocking, but
a summary judgment is not permissible here, for Franz' and
Dora's love was so true, so deep, that Kafka wished for nothing
more than to realize the ambition he had always set for himself,
even when he had thought it impossible:

He wanted to marry Dora, and had sent her pious father a letter in
which he had explained that, although he was not a practicing Jew
in her father's sense, he was nevertheless a "repentant one, seeking
'to return,'" and therefore might perhaps hope to be accepted into
the family of such a pious man (FK, 208).

Unfortunately Dora's father judged it well to consult a
"miracle-working" rabbi whose "oracular" response—in no way
ambiguous, alas—was a categorical rejection of the marriage. All
this was the result of mere chance, of course, but how in keeping
with the fatality that seems to have weighed upon Kafka's
destiny. In straying from Judaism, he had opposed his father.
When he turned back toward Judaism, it was his father who
strayed away from it. And now that he had broken all of the
inner and external obstacles to his marriage, it was the paterfamilias and the holy man who refused him the right to marry.
One can easily imagine what conclusions Kafka might have
drawn from this situation with respect to K.'s adventures: for
months the future had been adorned in a bridal gown, but the
ceremony was indefinitely put off by obscure powers that be.

Nevertheless, this was only the external, ritual aspect of the
drama. What was missing from Franz' and Dora's marriage?

Nothing except the approval and ceremonies of "others," for what makes a marriage is the consent of a man and a woman, and this consent had been given. Under the law of Paradise, Franz and Dora were married. In one sense, this state of affairs resulted from a strange set of conflicting circumstances, but it is singularly typical of Kafka's spirit. Placing himself simultaneously beyond ritual and the denial of ritual, Kafka reestablished direct contact with paradisiacal law.

It is not strange, therefore, that one should perceive that this "free union" corresponded to a new forward surge in Kafka's religious evolution. That this should happen is contrary to both the laws of ordinary probability and the Law of Moses, but the fact is there.

The rich treasure of Polish Jewish religious tradition that Dora was mistress of was a constant source of delight to Franz . . . (FK, 208).

And from Hasidism, the same enthusiasm for Judaism carried them towards Zionism. All that they had hitherto merely wished for and pondered over now seemed near to accomplishment. Like so many others who seek to return to their original sources, Dora and Franz longed to leave for Palestine in the Land of Canaan, the Promised Land. Dora would be a cook, Franz a waiter in a café.* Let who will laugh at this project. Had not the wealthy Vicomte de Foucauld left a few years earlier for the same land of Israel, in order to live and work there as a domestic servant?** Considering the vast differences between the two men, it is all the more striking to find in them an analagous desire to return, in poverty and as manual laborers, to the Kingdom of Israel.

From afar everything had been painstakingly prepared. Kafka's nascent return to Judaism had attracted him to the Berlin Jewish People's Home; "by chance" it was the Home that had led him to Dora, and it was with her that he found,

* Marthe Robert, Kafka, p. 49.
** See Michel Carrouges, Foucauld devant l'Afrique du Nord [trans. note].

mingled with the breath of love, the breath of Israel, stronger
and more alive than ever.

It was too late.

During the terrible Berlin winter and the hardships imposed
by that period of inflation, Kafka's illness reasserted itself and
his condition rapidly worsened to the critical stage. In March,
1924, only six months after his move to Berlin, Kafka was
obliged because of his health to return hastily to Prague, moving
then from sanatorium to clinic to sanatorium, the last time to
Kierling on the outskirts of Vienna. Dora, his family, his friends
all surrounded him with the best they could provide, but Destiny
is stronger than all else: Kafka died on June 3, 1924, at the end
of his fortieth year.

From one viewpoint there is nothing more disturbing—some
will say derisive—than this destiny of a man who found happiness, after forty years, only during the last year of his life. But
for those who see in him the heroic Kafka, penetrating into the
fissure of destruction towards the yoga of the indestructible, will
they not, on the contrary, be disappointed to see him return to
the familiar world of men? Perhaps, but that is unimportant.
This return was not a turning back, for from Kafka's own point
of view love was an integral part of the indestructible and of the
reintegration of mankind into Paradise. All the solitude and
implacable lucidity through which he had lived, far from being
demolished, was magnificently gathered together and transformed into happiness, the blossoming of the desert flower.

There in the pale light of death's dawning, everything neared
fulfillment—in the midst of things left unfulfilled. For during
Kafka's last two years the diaries were almost completely abandoned, and there exists no message from his final days that might
reveal what Kafka's final vision in the face of death may have
been.

Did he admit a little, a very little bit of hope, or a great deal
of hope? Kafka was to enter into the indestructible and decisive
consciousness, but he did not know what he would find there.

Kafka had enough genius to have invented a new Kabbala or

a new esoteric doctrine that might have far surpassed the con-
fusions of theosophy—and he knew it. But he did not do it. This
was not a failure on his part but a victory, for he knew better
than to become his own dupe. He did not pretend to transform
the modest allusions to the life hereafter that the human mind
is capable of discovering in this life into pseudo-revelations of
a life beyond this world. No gnosis and no yoga invented by
man has ever succeeded in forcing the secrets of death.

Yet he believed with all his being in the indestructible reality
of the spiritual world within and beyond the confines of the
sensual world. But what spiritual world?

Kafka departed from that sparse parcel of Canaan that was
his Judaic patrimony and set out for the farthest reaches of the
wilderness; but however far he went the indestructible outline of
Canaan, having become as infinitesimal as a star, shone on the
horizon with undiminished brilliance. Once again he set out in its
direction, but by another route where everything was changed.
He returned not as a captive but as a free man. In the multitude
of questions that he asked himself about the Old Testament, one
sees that in seeking to find the sources of Canaan's mystery,
Kafka only multiplied the enigmas. In the human memory of
Paradise and of Original Sin, two violently contradictory images
of the goodness and the wrath of God confront each other.
More profoundly contradictory is the bewildering image of
God as one who sets forth His Law and yet leaves in the hands
of His creatures the power to rebel. Even more profoundly
contradictory is the double image—without which all that pre-
cedes would be impossible—of God as one who reveals Himself
and yet does not reveal Himself, who fails to make Himself
unequivocally manifest before all His creatures. Between the
God of Genesis and the unknowable En-Sof* of the Kabbala
there is an opposition, but not an absolute separation. What
remains inexorably at the heart of the spiritual world is the
ambiguity of revelation, and, consequently, the fundamental

* *En-Sof:* In Kabbalistic doctrine, the absolutely infinite God [trans.
note].

ambiguity of man's destiny. During his entire life Kafka was as though entranced by this double ambiguity.

However, he did not remain transfixed; he really set out on a journey. He died in sight of the Promised Land of marriage and of the Land of Canaan which, for him, had come to mean one and the same thing, and to signify the indestructible presence of Paradise within the limits of immediate sensual reality. Precisely because he desired and contemplated their attainment, it can be said of Kafka what he said of Moses:

He is on the track of Canaan all his life; it is incredible that he should see the land only when on the verge of death. This dying vision of it can only be intended to illustrate how incomplete a moment is human life . . . Moses fails to enter Canaan not because his life is too short but because it is a human life (*DII*, 195–96).

To the very end of his tragic pilgrimage, Kafka wandered outside of all he desired and hoped for. He died just when he had at last arrived at the threshold of happiness, but he died with his face turned toward the Promised Land and Canaan.

In this act there was neither rebellion nor submissiveness, nor derision, nor chance, nor certainty, nor traditional faith, nor denial, but that incredible life force in our twilight world that bursts forth from the indestructible enigma of Israel, upon all peoples.

Was not Kafka, however, as reticent, as stubborn, as hostile perhaps as he was impassioned by Israel's appeal? This is a fact, and it is a contradiction, but it is not an anomaly.

Brod compares Kafka to Job (*FK*, 172). The comparison is not inaccurate, but it suggests only part of Kafka's enigma and tragedy. To evoke Job alone does not suffice; one must also recall Jonah, Balaam, David, a thousand other Israelites, and Abraham's grandson, Jacob, who changed his name and gave his new name to his whole race: since he was given the name Israel, his descendants became Israelites.

It happened on the night that Jacob spent beside the ford of Jabbok. Throughout the night Jacob struggled with an anonymous "someone," and at dawn, though his hip had been dislocated, Jacob still did not relax his grip; he demanded that his adversary give him his blessing. The latter refused to divulge his name, but agreed to bless Jacob, saying to him: "Thy name shall be called no more Jacob, but Israel: for as a prince hast thou power with God and with men, and hast prevailed" (Genesis, 32:28).

Israel had meant "God is strong" or "prevailing with God," but henceforth Israel also meant "contend with God." The people of the living God are also the people who "contend with God."

Vainly does one attempt to reduce that strange night of combat on the banks of the Jabbok to the level of human explanations. The mystery remains forever complete and insoluble. It is the mystery of the human condition and of the ambiguity of faith.

During the night, "someone" called the man Israel to a gigantic struggle. In the middle of the night, Kafka took up the same struggle. Kafka was a true son of Israel.

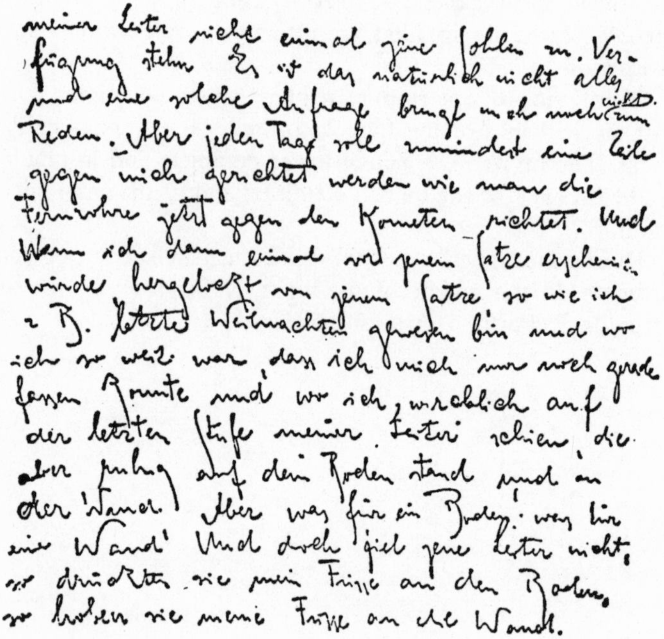
meiner Leiter nicht einmal jene Sohlen zu Verfügung stehn. Es ist das natürlich nicht alles und eine solche Anfrage bringt mich noch nicht zum Reden. Aber jeden Tag soll zumindest eine Zeile gegen mich gerichtet werden wie man die Fernrohre jetzt gegen den Kometen richtet. Und wenn ich dann einmal vor jenem Satze erscheinen würde hergelockt von jenem Satze, so wie ich z. B. letzte Weihnachten gewesen bin und wo ich so weit war, dass ich mich nur noch gerade fassen konnte und wo ich wirklich auf der letzten Stufe meiner Leiter schien, die aber ruhig auf dem Boden stand und an der Wand. Aber was für ein Boden! was für eine Wand! Und doch fiel jene Leiter nicht, so drückten sie meine Füsse an den Boden, so hoben sie meine Füsse an die Wand.

Example of Kafka's Handwriting

Graphological Analysis

Handwriting is a very complex expression of human nature. Every variation from the schoolroom model is a character index determined by the individuality of the person who is writing, and the most minuscule graphic element is a partial expression of that individuality. Of course, a small sample of handwriting is not enough; to make a detailed study, in order to grasp the total individuality, one needs several pages of original texts. Here we have had only a photographed document, not dated, and, later on, a signature. Here is what appeared evident to us before we knew the identity of the writer.

This handwriting reveals above all a vibrant, hypersensitive, quivering nature, a nature in which the sharpness of perception is such that a ray of light, the vibration of a wave, the reflection of an image, the slightest touch, constitute irresistible appeals to the emotive fluid, which reacts to every stimulus in a constant and reversible renewal of the sensations: a hyper-nervous, over-emotional, and tormented nature that burns with an interior fire and lives especially on the irrational and intuitive plane: an immense intuition, somewhat visionary.

Very artistic nature, cultivated, full of charm and radiance.

Poetic and literary vocation, especially an intellectual vocation.

The line of orientation is rather philosophic; whatever the writer's interests are, they are varied, even political. The writer has ideas, many ideas, and many sound ideas, for he has good judgment. He is endowed with a very intense, very affirmative, original personality. He is extremely individualistic.

The predominantly linear aspect of the handwriting (there are few rounded forms) indicates an inclination towards envisioning the essentiality of phenomena. Sensitivity and ideation are closely linked. Forces, impulses are transformed into thought by virtue of a strong need for objectivity and logic. An extremely keen mind; an especially abstractive activity of the intelligence.

The tendency to structure, the systematic concentration for which the entire energy is used, make him a dilettante thinker, like an artist, but a profound one who seeks the meaning of things up to the metaphysical plane. In fact, the tension, the simplicity, the strong vertical line in this handwriting, suggest the search for the *non-temporal*.

The only more open forms are the capital letters, the "B" especially (the symbol of the mother). This indicates the importance for the writer of hierarchies, values, the need to refer to themes of aristocratic grandeur, to guideline images. But these capitals are unfinished, sometimes narrow; there is a parental problem.

If hypersensitivity is keen, the emotional life is minimized, defended, unstable, reduced to perceptions, to impressions with which the writer identifies completely. Withdrawal, faculty of imitation and adaptiveness, pragmatic changeability, an aptitude for metamorphosing the self, for playing several roles, ambivalent character, torn between opposing poles, avid for affection, generosity, but also the *impossibility* of establishing a direct emotional contact—only indirectly, and by way of very complicated detours: there is in this almost an infirmity that has been conditioned by emotional insecurity during childhood.

This explains the inferiority complex, over-compensated in ambition, in self-insinuation, in the desire to shine. This explains the solitude, the profound duality, the incapacity to achieve in daily life certain morbid inclinations, and the quest for the inaccessible ideal towards which he flees from the real. But the writer is seeking the deep roots of his being in the unconscious. He is subject to states of depression. He is compelled by irrational forces—now towards the abyss, now towards the absolute. And since he is creative, he projects all his problems into his works. Emotional instability, physical activity, but also frail. On the other hand, a will of iron, an all-or-nothing outlook that forces him, that imposes on him a forward movement along very straight lines from which he does not deviate. Such compulsion can destroy vitality, can create a "pathos." There remains a very sure, instinctive strength of intention and beyond it, an insufficient experience of the real, an aspiration to attain the pure essence of things.   J. MONNOT

Opinions

Kafka, the subtle self-destroyer and endless hairsplitter.

R. M. ALBÉRÈS AND PIERRE DE BOISDEFFRE
Kafka, p. 48

√ He bends before an authority that denies him, although the way in which he bends is more violent than an outcry of affirmation; he bends in loving and in dying, while opposing the silence of love and death to what could not make him yield.

GEORGES BATAILLE
La Littérature et le mal, p. 182

Kafka's tales, in all of literature, are among the blackest, the most solidly bound to absolute disaster.

MAURICE BLANCHOT
La Part du feu, p. 18

Over the destiny of the average, contemporary man, of the passerby who hurries along parallel to the beating rain, in a light that does not vary beyond the dull shades of the cloth in a tailor's sample-book, Kafka sends fleeting, like a sudden gust of

wind, the question of all time: Where are we going, to what do
we owe allegiance, what is the law?

ANDRÉ BRETON
Anthologie de l'humour noir, p. 439

Without excluding more specific interpretations, which may
be completely valid, but which are subsumed within this very
comprehensive one as the inner compartments of a Chinese
puzzle are enclosed within the outer—this "Castle" to which K.
never gains admission, to which for some incomprehensible
reason he can never even get near, is much the same thing as what
theologians call "grace," the divine guidance of human destiny
(the village), the effectual cause of all chances, mysterious dis-
pensations, favours and punishments, the unmerited and the
unattainable, the "Non liquet" written over the life of every-
body. In *The Trial* and *The Castle*, then, are represented the two
manifested forms of the Godhead (in the sense of *The Cabbala*),
justice and grace.

MAX BROD
The Castle, "Note," p. 444

Man then concerns himself with hope. But this is not his business. His business is to turn away from subterfuge. Now, it is this
that I find at the end of the vehement trial that Kafka institutes
against the entire universe. His incredible verdict acquits, in the
end, this hideous and overwhelming world where even moles
dabble in hope.

ALBERT CAMUS
Le Mythe de Sisyphe, p. 185

I reread Kafka's *The Trial* with even keener admiration, if
that is possible, than when I first discovered this amazing
book . . .

ANDRÉ GIDE
Journal, 28 August 1940

Confronted with this drama preconceived by some kind of unnamed power [*The Trial*], we have the right to wonder if Kafka did not wish to re-stage, in making use of a purely social subject, the cruellest farce that humanity has ever been the victim of: the story of original sin.

GEORGES HENEIN
In *Clé*, No. 2, Revue de la F.I.A.R.I., 1939

All Kafka's work emits an air of expectation of the messianic Kingdom. For him, complete physical recovery, and with it the justified enjoyment of good health, will coincide with the coming of the Kingdom, and, since the Kingdom has not yet come for anyone, no one is able to overestimate what still eludes all of us: then, health will be holiness.

PIERRE KLOSSOWSKI
"Introduction"
F. Kafka, *Journal intime* (fragments), p. 11

When Max Brod and others after him would have us see in *The Castle* no more than the drama of accession to that grace which is refused for no reason and which one finally obtains when one no longer hopes for it, we feel that we have been cheated.

CLAUDE-EDMONDE MAGNY
Les Sandales d'Empédocle, p. 173

I have nothing to say of Kafka, if not that he is one of the rarest and greatest writers of our time . . . If he shows us human life perpetually troubled by an impossible transcendence, it is because he believed in the existence of that transcendence. Simply, it is beyond our attainment.

JEAN-PAUL SARTRE
Situations I, p. 139

He never uses words for their own sake. He is not a bizarre

writer in the sense that bizarreness is an arbitrary preference, or even a taste for the strange. If his work is strange, it is so because of its depth, because he sees from an angle peculiar to him things of which we thought we were aware as a matter of routine, and that he reveals to us that we were not aware of them. An explorer is not bizarre because he brings back from the tropics monsters never before seen. Kafka is the opposite of an artificial writer.

ALEXANDRE VIALETTE
quoted by Marthe Robert in *Kafka*, p. 272

Make no mistake: if Kafka created a hell, it was warranted in his eyes by the conception of a paradise.

JEAN WAHL
Petite histoire de l'existentialisme, p. 129

One has just been sent out as a biblical dove, has found nothing green, and slips back into the darkness of the arch [sic].

FRANZ KAFKA
Letters to Milena, p. 208

Chronology

1883   Franz Kafka is born on July 3, in Prague, the son of Hermann Kafka, a wholesale merchant, and Julie Löwy Kafka. Franz was the eldest child, followed by two brothers who died very young, and three sisters, of whom Ottla, the youngest, was Franz's favorite.

1893   Begins studies at the German Gymnasium in Prague.

1901   Enters the German University to study law.

1906   Receives his doctorate in jurisprudence on June 8. On October 1, begins obligatory one-year practice at the criminal and civil courts in Prague. In 1906–07, begins his first short stories.

1907   On October 1, begins work at the *Assicurazioni Generali*, an insurance company.

1908   In July, takes a position with the semi-nationalized Workers' Accident Insurance Institute.

1909   Publication of extracts from "Description of a Struggle" in the literary periodical *Hyperion*.

1910   Begins the *Diaries*.

1911   Meeting with Löwy and his Yiddish theatrical troop (Brod places this event in 1910).

1912   Kafka begins *Amerika*. On August 13, at Max Brod's, he meets F.B. During the night of September 22–23, he writes *The Judgment*, at a single sitting, during an extraordinary state of exaltation.

1913   Publication of "The Stoker," the first chapter of *Amerika*. Publication of *The Judgment* in the literary yearbook *Ar-*

kadia. Publication of *Meditation.* Writes *The Metamorphosis,* begun probably in 1912.

1914 Engagement to F.B. in Berlin, in May; the engagement is broken in July. Kafka, a civil servant, is not mobilized with the army. In August, begins *The Trial,* then interrupts it in order to write the first draft of *The Penal Colony.*

1915 Renews his engagement to F.B. Returns to *The Trial.* The first version of "Investigations of a Dog" dates from this period. In October, receives the Fontane Prize for "The Stoker."

1916 Franz and F. meet during their vacation at Marienbad. Writes "A Country Doctor" and several other tales.

1917 Second engagement to F.B. in July. Coughs up blood for the first time in August. Spends sick leave in Zürau at the home of his sister, Ottla. In December, the final break with F.B.

1918 Begins study of Hebrew. Writes *The Great Wall of China.*

1919 Writes the *Letter to his Father* in November. Publication of *A Country Doctor.* Short-lived engagement to Julie Wohryzek.

1920 Stay in Meran, Austria (Merano, Italy). Meets Milena Jesenská.

1921 Stay in a sanatorium in the Tatra Mountains. Returns to Prague.

1922 Writes *The Castle.* Writes "Josephine the Singer" and "A Hunger Artist" (Brod dates composition of these two tales in 1923).

1923 May 9, the last letter to Milena. June 12, the last page of the *Diaries.* July, vacation at Müritz. Meets Dora Dymant. August, returns to Prague, resigns his job, and decides to leave Prague to go live with Dora. September, in Berlin with Dora.

1924 Kafka's health grows worse during the winter. In March, return to Prague where Dora joins him. Kafka is moved to a clinic in Vienna, then to the sanatorium at Kierling. Corrects proofs of *A Hunger Artist.* Kafka dies at the sanatorium on June 3, and is buried in the family tomb in the Jewish Cemetery in Prague.

Select Bibliography*

* TRANSLATOR'S NOTE: Listed here are those items that M. Carrouges includes in his bibliography. In the case of Kafka's works and works on Kafka that were originally written in German, I have listed the English rather than the French versions. I have retained the French titles of books and articles written originally in French. English translations of the French entries, where they are available, are listed immediately following the French title. The critical remarks following certain of the entries are those of M. Carrouges.

ENGLISH TRANSLATIONS OF KAFKA'S WORKS

Amerika. Trans. Willa and Edwin Muir. New York: Doubleday, 1946 ("Afterword" by Max Brod).

The Castle. Trans. Edwin Muir. London: Martin Secker, 1930 ("Afterword" by Max Brod).

Dearest Father. Trans. Ernst Kaiser and Eithne Wilkins. New York: Schocken, 1954. In addition to the "Letter to His Father," this volume contains: "Wedding Preparations in the Country," "Reflections on Sin, Suffering, Hope, and the True Way," "The Eight Octavo Notebooks," "Fragments from Notebooks and Loose Pages," and "Paralipomena." The "Letter to His Father" has been published separately in a paperback edition (New York: Schocken, 1966).

Diaries: 1910–1913. Trans. Joseph Kresh. Ed. Max Brod. New York: Schocken, 1948.

Diaries: 1914–1923. Trans. Martin Greenberg and Hannah Arendt. Ed. Max Brod. New York: Schocken, 1949.

The Great Wall of China. Trans. Willa and Edwin Muir. New York: Schocken, 1946. In addition to the title story, this volume contains: "Investigations of a Dog," "The Burrow," "The Giant Mole," "The Hunter Gracchus," "The Married Couple," "My Neighbor," "A Common Confusion," "The Bridge," "The Bucket Rider," "A Sport," "The Knock at the Manor Gate," "The City Coat of Arms," "The Silence of the Sirens," "Prometheus," "The Truth about Sancho Panza," "The Problem of our Laws," "On Parables," "A Little Fable," "He," and "Reflections on Sin, Pain, Hope, and the True Way."

Letters to Milena. Trans. Tania and James Stern. Ed. Willi Haas. New York: Schocken, 1962.

Metamorphosis. Trans. A. D. Lloyd. New York: Vanguard Press, 1946.

The Penal Colony. Trans. Willa and Edwin Muir. New York: Schocken, 1961. In addition to the title story, this volume contains: "Conversation with the Supplicant," "Meditation," "The Judgment," "The Metamorphosis," "A Country Doctor," "A Hunger Artist," and an appendix comprising: "The First Long Train Journey" by Kafka and Max Brod, "The Aeroplanes at Brescia," "Three Critical Pieces," and an epilogue by Max Brod.

The Trial. Trans. Willa and Edwin Muir. Rev. ed. with additional materials translated by E. M. Butler. New York: Alfred Knopf, 1960. An appendix to this volume contains: "Unfinished Chapters," "Passages Deleted by the Author," and "Postscripts" by Max Brod.

Parables (New York: Schocken, 1946) and *Selected Short Stories of Franz Kafka* (New York: Modern Library, 1952) contain selections from Kafka's works.

Books about Kafka

Brod, Max. *Franz Kafka*. Second, Enlarged Edition. Trans. G. Humphreys Roberts and Richard Winston. New York: Schocken, 1960. Written by an intimate friend of Kafka, this biography is basic. However, a new, more methodical, and still more complete biography would be desirable.

Carrouges, Michel. *Kafka*. Paris: Labergerie, 1948. Although this work is completely out of print, we mention it in order to point out that we have reworked it from top to bottom in the present book, but that, for lack of space, we have omitted its chapter on the art of Kafka.

Janouch, Gustav. *Conversations with Kafka: Notes and Reminiscences*. Trans. Gronwy Rees. Introduction by Max Brod. New York: Praeger, 1953. Excellent notes set down after discussions with Kafka by one of his friends.

Nemeth, André. *Kafka ou le mystère juif*. Paris: Jean Vigneau, 1947. A number of interesting observations.

Robert, Marthe. *Introduction à la lecture de Kafka*. Paris: Sagittaire, 1946.

Robert, Marthe. *Kafka*. Paris: Gallimard, 1960. Questionable views concerning Kafka's use of symbolism in no way detract from the value of the greater part of this fine work, which contains many interesting remarks, beautiful iconography, and a vast bibliography.

ARTICLES ABOUT KAFKA

Bataille, Georges, "Kafka," in *La Littérature et le mal*. Paris: Gallimard, 1957, pp. 161–80.

Blanchot, Maurice, "Kafka," in *La Part du feu*. Paris: Gallimard, 1949.

Breton, André, "Kafka," in *Anthologie de l'humour noir*. Paris: Jean-Jacques Pauvert, [1966], pp. 439–60.

Camus, Albert, "L'Espoir et l'absurde dans l'oeuvre de Franz Kafka," in *Le Mythe de Sisyphe*. Paris: Gallimard, 1942, pp. 169–85.

Carrive, Jean, "Préface" to *La Muraille de Chine*. Paris: Seghers, 1948.

Carrouges, Michel, "La Machine célibataire selon Franz Kafka et Marcel Duchamp," in *Les Machines célibataires*. Paris: Arcanes, 1954. This article also appears in *Mercure de France*, CCCXV, No. 1066 (1952), 262–81. [See footnote on page 42.]

Klossowski, Pierre, "Introduction au *Journal intime* de Franz Kafka," in *Cahiers du Sud*, XXII, No. 270 (1945), 151–71.

Magny, Claude-Edmonde, "Kafka ou l'écriture de l'absurde," in *Les Sandales d'Empédocle*. Neuchâtel: La Baconnière, 1945, pp. 173–266.

——, "The Objective Depiction of Absurdity," in *The Kafka Problem*. Ed. Angel Flores. New York: New Directions, 1946, pp. 75–96.

Sartre, Jean-Paul, "Aminadab," in *Situations I*. Paris: Gallimard, 1947, pp. 122–42.

Wahl, Jean, "Kafka et Kierkegaard," in *Petite histoire de l'existentialisme*. Paris: Club Maintenant, 1947.

——, "Kierkegaard and Kafka," in *The Kafka Problem*. Ed. Angel Flores. New York: New Directions, 1946, pp. 262–75.

Index